AFTER-DINNER
DECLARATIONS

AFTER-DINNER DECLARATIONS

NICANOR PARRA

TRANSLATED AND WITH AN INTRODUCTION BY
DAVE OLIPHANT

HOST PUBLICATIONS
AUSTIN, TEXAS

Host Publications, Inc. 277 Broadway, Suite 210, New York, NY 10007

Layout and Design:	Joe Bratcher & Anand Ramaswamy
Cover Photo of Nicanor Parra:	Claudio Pérez
Cover Design:	Anand Ramaswamy

First Edition

Library of Congress Cataloging-in-Publication Data

Parra, Nicanor, 1914-
[Discursos de sobremesa. English & Spanish]
After-dinner declarations / Nicanor Parra ; translated and with an introduction by Dave Oliphant.
    p. cm.
Summary: "[Bilingual Spanish/English edition of the Chilean poetry collection by Nicanor Parra]"--Provided by publisher.
ISBN-13: 978-0-924047-62-6 (hardcover : alk. paper)
ISBN-10: 0-924047-62-3 (hardcover : alk. paper)
ISBN-13: 978-0-924047-63-3 (pbk. : alk. paper)
ISBN-10: 0-924047-63-1 (pbk. : alk. paper)
I. Oliphant, Dave. II. Title.
PQ8097.P322.D5713 2008
861'.62--dc22

                                                    2008028565

TABLE OF CONTENTS

INTRODUCTION

To translate Nicanor Parra's *Discursos de sobremesa* as *After-Dinner Declarations* cannot begin to suggest the true nature of this self-proclaimed antipoet's collection of five "verse" speeches, delivered on five different occasions during the 1990s. Originally I had thought to title the book *After-Dinner Speeches*, but Parra himself preferred a translation of his "discursos" as "discourses," "declarations," or "statements." To me "discourses" sounded too formal and "statements" too flat, whereas the word "speeches" seemed more "the way we speak," in keeping with Parra's own position that poetry should be written in the language of the street. However, after considerable difficulty in deciding, I at last concluded that in fact "declarations" came the closest to characterizing Parra's antipoetic pronouncements, his diatribes and eulogies, his quipping challenges to those satisfied with the status quo or even, through graft and greed, bent on the destruction of the environment and life on earth as we know it.

To my mind, not even Parra's Spanish title for his "antispeeches" can indicate the wealth of political, religious, literary, social, philosophical, and personal concerns, insights, and witty satires in the 235 individual "antipoems" that make up his five "discursos." Perhaps taken altogether, the various dictionary definitions of "discursos" (talks, discourses, orations, and speeches), plus Parra's "statements" and "declarations," can furnish a fuller notion of the antipoet's broad spectrum of ideas and idioms. His speeches are indeed filled with "declarations" (of independence) on a wide range

i

of pressing issues, with one of these being his assertion that the only solution to our economic and ecological problems is the Mapuche Indians' form of subsistence living. Just to know the occasions that inspired the antipoet's five "discursos" reveals the far-reaching features of his creative writing. In 1991 he was awarded the Juan Rulfo Prize by the Mexican government; in 1993 he appeared before the Congress of the Theater of Nations on the birthday of William Shakespeare; also in 1993 he paid a centennial-year tribute to Vicente Huidobro, his fellow Chilean-born poet/antipoet, at the site of this "French" Creationist's home in Cartagena, located just across the bay from Parra's own beach home at Las Cruces; in 1996 the Universidad de Concepción conferred on him an Honorary Doctorate; and in 1997, at the Universidad Austral in Valdivia, he rendered homage to Chilean writer and educator Luis Oyarzún, his friend since their days at the Barros Arana secondary school and in the Pedagogical Department of the Universidad de Chile, both in Santiago.

If the title of this book has been for me a matter of substantial self-debate as a translator, it is nothing compared with my agonizing over the Chilean's colloquialisms, for which it has been a constant test of my memory and imagination to come up with similar or equivalent turns of phrase. Despite having frequently been dissatisfied with my final choices, I am, I believe, the better man for having struggled with Parra's apt locutions, since I know for certain that I have learned to appreciate more than ever his antipoetic art. I can only hope that my efforts will approximate for readers something of Don Nicanor's linguistic brilliance and logical ingenuity.

A few examples of the antipoet's wordplay may help indicate some of the difficulties that I faced as translator. In the Oyarzún speech, Parra changes *peda* or *paeda* in the Greek word pedagogy or pedagogical (Spanish "pedagogía" or "pedagógico") to "piedra," the Spanish for stone, rock, or pebble. In this case, my translation attempts to reproduce, through "pebble," Parra's triple entendre in "piedragógico," by means of the portmanteau "Pebblegogy." Along with "piedragógico" in the Oyarzún speech, Parra also combines his own name with the word "preparado" to extend or multiply the meanings, so that even single words ("piedragógico" or "pebblegogy" and "preparrado" or "preparraed") are "loaded" with antipoetic thought. The very title of the Oyarzún "declaration" derives from a popular Chilean joke in which a speaker claims that he "has not come prepared" to say anything but then pulls out and begins to read from a lengthy speech. To alert the reader to Parra's omnipresent puns and allusions, I have appended explanatory notes, but not for every instance of wordplay or historical reference. My explanatory comments are preceded by the phrase "translator's note," to distinguish them from the antipoet's own notes, which add informational or satirical asides to his poems in order to clarify who is who or, once again, to extend his themes and meanings.

In 2008, Parra continues at the age of 94 to amaze his admirers and to confound his critics, just as his *Discursos de sobremesa* did when all five of his "after-dinner declarations" appeared together for the first time in 2006 from Chile's Ediciones Universidad Diego Portales. And this had been true of Parra's earlier books published over a period of 68 years, beginning with his 1938 *Cancionero sin nombre* (*Unnamed Songs*), followed in 1954 by his revolutionary *Poemas y antipoemas* (*Poems and Antipoems* in its 1966 bilingual edition edited by Miller Williams for New Directions), and to mention but two of the later collections, his *Sermones y prédicas del Cristo de Elqui* of 1972 (reissued in an expanded edition in 2007), with its English title of *The Sermons and Preachings of the Christ of Elqui* having been given by Edith Grossman to a group of her 1977 translations, and in 2005 Parra's *Lear rey & mendigo*, his own translation of Shakespeare's *King Lear*.

Parra has long been a serious student of Shakespeare; partly this is because he considers the Bard the first antipoet. Among various reasons for the Chilean seeing in Shakespeare an antipoetic forebear is the fact that the Englishman's plays do not take sides, but rather present the pros and cons of every type of person and situation. Also, for Parra, Hamlet exemplifies the antipoetic position par excellence; that is, the Prince is, in Parra's words, the "Champion of Methodical Doubt," as the Chilean states in his "How Right Was the Owl When She Said," as translated by Liz Werner in *Antipoems: How to look better & feel great*, published in 2004 by New Directions. Hamlet's skeptical attitude is one that Parra has cultivated throughout his own writings, and as with so many of the antipoet's themes, each time that one reappears it comes with a slightly different twist. Here, for example, in the "Happy Birthday" / "Caupolicán Speech," the Prince answers the telephone and identifies himself as "one ill with methodical doubt."

From one speech to another, Parra at times repeats certain key declarations, especially his warnings against pollution and over-development that have led to the decimation of marine life and old-growth forests. But more than repetition, the antipoet's work in general, and his *After-Dinner Declarations* in particular, reveals his enduring, unbounded inventiveness, as he moves from one topic to another, discovering between them unexpected connections, as when he links Rulfo's novel, *Pedro Páramo*, with *Hamlet*, or finds Shakespeare and Cervantes to be two names for the same man. Each of the five speeches develops something of a narrative line, with "diversions" from it at times for vignettes on Argentine author Jorge Luis Borges, the Pope, or the crucifixion of Christ, the latter stumbled onto by a narrator who observes it "merely" out of curiosity. Parra's religious views run the gamut from amusement and ironic detachment to indignant sermons delivered by his alter ego, the Christ of Elqui, the itinerant preacher who, in his Quijote-like judgments, offers moral precepts within seemingly the most unlikely contexts.

Although Parra's five poem-speeches often concern his concept of antipoetry, mainly as it contrasts with the work of other literary figures, they also touch on such perennial motifs as ecology, human rights and responsibilities, philosophy (from Zeno of Elea and Plato to Friedrich Nietzsche, Max Stirner, Martin Heidegger, and Jacques Derrida), and math and science, the latter owing to his work as a professor of physics trained at Brown and Oxford universities. In the Bío Bío speech, Parra even manages to satirize, by way of his honorary doctorate, both professors and the medical profession, aiming his barbed witticisms at pedantic doctors of philosophy and the "Health Business." In this and the other "declarations," Parra also rings his changes on songs or popular sayings. In the same "doctor" discourse, the antipoet quotes a type of Mother Goose rhyme about little chicks whose cheeping in Spanish comes out as "pío pío." But for the occasion of this speech, as might be expected, Parra converts the sounds of the chicks into Bío Bío, the name of the Chilean river that flows through the southern city of Concepción, where he declaimed or harangued with tongue in cheek on receiving his *Doctorado Honoris Causa*.

In the Huidobro tribute, Parra works into his recapitulation of the "guerrilla" warfare among three Chilean poets of the 1930s (Huidobro, Pablo Neruda, and Pablo de Rokha) a number of songs and poems, applying them to his storyline for purposes of siding, unShakespeare-like, with Vicente, his favored "mentor." (A Whitman enthusiast, Parra would probably say of his favoritism, "Do I contradict myself? . . . I am large, I contain multitudes.") Also in the Huidobro eulogy, as in all of Parra's verse orations, he reveals his close reading of his "rivals," not only their poetry, but with the Big Three the history of their bitter brawls on the printed page. By way of acknowledging his indebtedness to Huidobro, Parra even "lifts" the entire first stanza from his fellow Chilean's "Monument to the Sea" and reproduces it nearly verbatim as the final stanza of his own "Also Sprach Altazor." The one change Parra makes is to add the letter "i" to Huidobro's word *traductor*, whereby the eulogist creates another of his neologisms, *traiductor,* which in my English version becomes "transla(trai)tor."

In the Rulfo and Bío Bío declarations, Parra has conceived a new, or revived a traditional, genre for his antipoetry: the address given on receiving an honor or award, which, in the antipoet's case, he finds so undeserved, and for which he remains ironically speechless, with no words to express his gratitude and disbelief. In the Rulfo "discurso" and elsewhere, the Chilean often turns his satire on himself, as when he speaks of working on the last "bad" speech of the twentieth century and the first "good" speech of the twenty-first, unable to decide which page goes with which speech. Whatever may be the best English title for Nicanor Parra's book of antipoetic homilies, maxims, jeremiads, homages, mathematical puns, and literary histories, the nonagenarian's entertaining and enlightening perspectives on the modern world are both trenchant oratory, in his own inventive type of verse, and forensic wordplay that goes beyond fun and games to confront some of the most serious problems of our day, doing so by pulling no punches and calling, as he loves to declare in one of his many epigrammatic expressions, an ace an ace. Once more, I can only hope that my "antitranslations" have captured something of the ingenious public utterance of this authentic, unaging antipoet.

– *Dave Oliphant, 2008*

DISCURSOS DE SOBREMESA

AFTER-DINNER DECLARATIONS

MAI MAI PEÑI

MAI MAI PEÑI

Nos salvamos juntos
o nos hundimos separados
(Juan Rulfo, *México y los mexicanos*)

We survive together
or each one sinks alone
(Juan Rulfo, *Mexico and the Mexicans*)

I

SEÑORA CLARA APARICIO

Vi(u)da de Rulfo
Distinguidas autoridades
Señoras y señores:

Un amigo que acaba de morir
Me sugirió la idea
De renunciar al proyecto de discurso académico
Basándose en el hecho
De que ya nadie cree en las ideas:

Fin de la historia
Arte y filosofía x el suelo

Lo que debes hacer
Es leer tus antipoemas me dijo Carlos Ruiz-Tagle
De preferencia
Los que se relacionan con la muerte
La muerte tiene la vara muy alta en México:
Rulfo te aplaudirá desde la tumba

I

MRS. CLARA APARICIO

Widowlife of Rulfo
Distinguished authorities
Ladies and Gentlemen:

A friend who has just died
Suggested to me the notion
That I forget about giving an academic speech
Basing it on the fact
That nowadays no one believes in ideas:

End of history
Art and philosophy toppled

What you should do
Is read your antipoems Carlos Ruiz-Tagle said to me
Preferibly
Those that are closely connected with death
In Mexico death has a lot of pull:
Rulfo will applaud you from his grave

II

HAY DIFERENTES TIPOS DE DISCURSOS

Qué duda cabe
El discurso patriótico sin ir + lejos

Otro discurso digno de mención
Es el discurso que se borra a sí mismo:

Mímica x un lado
Voz y palabra x otro

Vale la pena recordar también
El discurso huidobriano de una sola palabra
Repetida hasta las náuseas
En todos los tonos imaginables

El lector estará de acuerdo conmigo no obstante
En que se reducen a dos
Todos los tipos de discursos posibles:

Discursos buenos y discursos malos

El discurso ideal
Es el discurso que no dice nada
Aunque parezca que lo dice todo
Mario Moreno me dará la razón

II

THERE ARE DIFFERENT TYPES OF SPEECHES

No question about that
The patriotic speech to look no further

Another type worth mentioning
Is the speech that erases itself:

Pantomime on one side
Voice and word on the other

Also worth recalling
Is the Huidobrian speech of just one word
Repeated ad nauseam
In every imaginable tone

Even so the reader will agree with me
That all kinds of speeches
Come down to two possible types:

Good speeches and bad speeches

The ideal speech
Is the one that doesn't say a thing
Even though it seems like it says it all
Mario Moreno will side with me*

*Translator's note: the real name of Mexican film star Cantinflas.

III

DE HECHO YO ESTABA PREPARÁNDOME

Para pronunciar dos discursos a falta de uno
Como buen discípulo de Macedonio Fernández

x una parte proyectaba pronunciar
El último discurso malo del siglo XX
Y a renglón seguido
El primer discurso bueno del siglo XXI
Cuando me crucé con Carlos Ruiz-Tagle
Que cayó muerto en la vía pública
Mientras se dirigía a su oficina

Pergeñar el primer discurso bueno
Para un orador nato como el que habla
En la práctica no resulta nada del otro mundo
Basta con plagiar al pie de la letra
A Hitler a Stalin al Sumo Pontífice

Lo difícil es redactar el último malo
Porque no faltará alguien
Que salga con otro peor

Estoy sentado al escritorio
A mi izquierda los manuscritos del último discurso malo
A mi derecha los del primer discurso bueno
Acabo de redactar una página
Mi problema es el siguiente
Dónde la deposito madre mía!
A la izquierda? a la derecha?

Caution
El cadáver de Marx aún respira

III

IN FACT I WAS PREPARING MYSELF

For delivering two speeches for lack of one
Like a good disciple of Macedonio Fernández

On one hand I was planning to give
The last bad speech of the twentieth century
And in the next breath
The first good speech of the twenty-first
When I ran across Carlos Ruiz-Tagle
Who dropped dead on the street
On the way to his office

To write the first good speech
For a born orator like the one who's speaking
Is not a big deal
Just plagiarize faithfully
From Hitler Stalin and the Highest Pontiff

The hard part is to put into writing the last bad speech
Because there will always be someone
Who will come along with one that's worse

I'm seated at my desk
To my left the manuscripts of the last bad speech
On my right the ones for the first good speech
I have just finished writing a page
My problem is the following
For heaven's sake where do I put it!
On the left? on the right?

Caution
Marx's corpse is breathing yet

IV

A DECIR VERDAD

Uno de los discursos posibles
Podría empezar así:

Señoras y señores
Antes de proceder a dar las gracias
x este premio tan inmerecido
Quiero pedir licencia para leer
Unas notas tomadas al vuelo
Mientras me acostumbraba a la noticia
Lo que no quiere decir
Que no pudiera comenzar asá:

Señoras y señores:
Por lo común los discursos de sobremesa
Son buenos pero largos
El mío será malo pero corto
Cosa
Que no debiera sorprender a nadie
Soy incapaz de juntar dos ideas
Es x eso que me declaro poeta
De lo contrario hubiera sido político
O filósofo o comerciante

IV

TO TELL THE TRUTH

One possible speech
Could begin like this:

Ladies & gentlemen
Before proceeding to thank you
For this honor so undeserved
I ask that you allow me to read
Some notes taken on the fly
As I was getting used to the news
Which doesn't mean
That it couldn't start like this:

Ladies & gentlemen:
In general after-dinner speeches
Are good but long
My own will be bad but short
Something
That shouldn't surprise anyone
I'm incapable of putting two thoughts together
It's for that reason that I declare that I'm a poet
Otherwise I would have been a politician
Or a philosopher or a businessman

V

PARA ENTRAR EN CONFIANZA

Permítaseme recordar unos versos de ciego
Que encontré en una tumba abandonada
Hacen sus buenos años
                 en el norte de Chile↑
En Monte Grande para ser + preciso
Me parece que vienen al caso:

      Yo soy Lucila Alcayaga
      Alias Gabriela Mistral
      Primero me gané el Nobel
      Y después el Nacional

      A pesar de que estoy muerta
      Me sigo sintiendo mal
      Porque nunca me dieron
      El Premio Municipal

El poeta como guía turístico dirán ustedes
El poeta como maestro de ceremonias
El poeta como operador cibernético:
Tal cual

Y ahora cumpliré la palabra empeñada
Ante mi gran amigo Carlos Ruiz-Tagle
Que cayó muerto en la vía pública
Mientras se dirigía a su domicilio

Todos vamos en esa dirección

V

TO WARM UP

Let me recall some anonymous verses
That I found in an abandoned tomb
A good many years ago
                              up in the north of Chile↑
To be precise on Monte Grande
To me they seem apropos:

>I am Lucila Alcayaga
>Alias Gabriela Mistral
>First I won the Nobel Prize
>And then the National

>Even though I am dead
>I go on feeling just awful
>Because they never gave me
>The Municipal award

The poet as tourist guide you will say
The poet as master of ceremonies
The poet as cybernetic operator:
That's the way it is

And now I will keep the promise
Made to my great friend Carlos Ruiz-Tagle
Who dropped dead in the street
While on his way home

We're all headed in that same direction

VI

PEDRO PÁRAMO

Guadalajara en un llano
México en una laguna

1

No pienses más en mí Susana
Te lo suplico
Sabes perfectamente que estoy muerto
30 años que llevo bajo tierra
Tu segundo marido sufre mucho por ti
Terminará volviéndose loco
Si continúas tú delirando conmigo
Ordenará matarte seguramente
Sabes que es un hombre decidido
Nunca lo llamas por su propio nombre
No puede ser Susana
No puede ser
En vez de Pedro le dices Florencio
Y en el momento más inoportuno...

2

Yo también estoy muerta Florencio
Tengo la boca llena de tierra
Pero me es imposible olvidarme de ti
Tú me descuartizaste
No siento nada por Pedro Páramo
Si me casé con él fue de puro miedo
Tú lo sabes perfectamente bien
Nos hubiera hecho matar a todos

VI

PEDRO PÁRAMO

> *Guadalajara on a plain*
> *Mexico on a lake*

1

Don't think about me anymore Susana
I beg of you
You know perfectly well that I'm dead
For 30 years I've been in the grave
Your second husband suffers over you so
If you continue raving on about me
He will end up going insane
For sure he'll order you put to death
You know he's a determined man
You never call him by his proper name
It can't be Susana
It can't be
Instead of Pedro you call him Florencio
At the most inopportune times...

2

I too am dead Florencio
My mouth is filled with earth
But it's impossible to forget you
You cut me into little pieces
I don't feel a thing for Pedro Páramo
If I married him it was purely out of fear
You know only too well
He would have had us all killed

3

Susana amor mío!

4

Te repito Susana
Que no me digas más Bartolomé
Soy tu padre
Bartolomé San Juan
Y tú eres mi hija legítima

Acaban de matarme Susana
Por orden de tu propio marido
Celos...
Alguien le dijo que éramos amantes
Sólo quería despedirme de ti
Perdona que te importune
Mi cadáver está a medio camino
Entre Sayula y Comala me oyes?
Ay!
Los zopilotes ya me arrancaron los ojos
Si te parece da cuenta a la comandancia
Para que se me entierre como es debido

3

Susana my love!

4

I tell you again Susana
Don't call me Bartolomé
I am your father
Bartolomé San Juan
And you are my legitimate daughter

They have just killed me Susana
On the orders of your own husband
Jealousy…
Someone told him we were lovers
I simply wanted to say goodbye
Forgive me for bothering you so
My corpse lies in the middle of the road
Between Sayula and Comala do you hear me?
Yow!
The buzzards just tore out my eyes
If you don't mind notify the district command
So they will bury me properly

VII

NO COMETERÉ LA TORPEZA

De ponerme a elogiar a Juan Rulfo
Sería como ponerse a regar el jardín
En un día de lluvia torrencial

Una sola verdad de Perogrullo:
Perfección enigmática
No conozco otro libro + terrible

Pedro Páramo dice Borges
Es una de las obras cumbres
De la literatura de todos los tiempos

Y yo le encuentro toda la razón

VII

I WON'T BE SO STUPID

As to eulogize Juan Rulfo
It would be like watering the garden
On a day of torrential rain

Just one truism:
Enigmatic perfection
I don't know a more terrible book

Borges says Pedro Páramo
Is one of the greatest literary works
Of all times

And I think he's totally right

VIII

RULFO NOS DA UNA IMAGEN DE MÉXICO

Los demás se reducen a describir el país
A eso se refiere Paz
Cuando *digo* que Juan hay un solo

VIII

RULFO GIVES US AN IMAGE OF MEXICO

The rest are reduced to describing the countryside
That's what Paz means
When *I say* there's just one Juan

IX

NI MACEDONIO FUE TAN ARGENTINO

Tan chileno
    tan indio
        tan peruano
Tan boliviano tan ecuatoriano
Tan auténticamente mexicano
Los entendidos tienen razón esta vez

Otro camino + directo no hay

IX

NOT EVEN MACEDONIO WAS SO ARGENTINIAN

So Chilean
     so Indian
          so Peruvian
So Bolivian so Ecuadorian
So authentically Mexican
This time the experts are right

There's no route more direct

X

FUMABA TANTO O MÁS QUE LA MISTRAL

Algo que a mí me pone los pelos de punta
Soy asmático de nacimiento
Por eso nunca pude hablar con él

Se me acercó una vez en Viña del Mar
A felicitarme x un poema que no era mío
No supe qué decirle
Me confundí
Y el pobre Juan también se confundió
Primera y última vez
No volvimos a vernos nunca +
Hasta este momento
En que él me sonríe desde Comala

X

HE SMOKED AS MUCH IF NOT MORE THAN MISTRAL

Which makes my skin crawl
I'm asthmatic from birth
For that reason I could never talk with him

He came up to me one time in Viña del Mar
To congratulate me on a poem that wasn't mine
I didn't know what to say to him
I was all confused
And poor Juan was perplexed as well
First and last time
We never saw one another ever again
Until this moment
When he smiles at me from Comala

XI

GENTE + PREPARADA QUE NOSOTROS

Ha dicho que Rulfo viene del Norte
Discrepo
Rulfo viene del Sur
Rulfo viene directamente del vientre materno
Rulfo viene del fondo de sí mismo
De Jalisco
    de Mérida
       de Guadalajara
Lo siento mucho Mister No Sé Cuánto
Rulfo no viene: va
Rulfo viene de vuelta de todos los archipiélagos

XI

PEOPLE SHARPER THAN WE ARE

Have said that Rulfo comes from the North
I disagree
Rulfo comes from the South
Rulfo comes straight from the maternal womb
Rulfo comes from deep within himself
From Jalisco
         from Mérida
                  from Guadalajara
I'm very sorry Mister So-and-so
Rulfo doesn't come: he goes
Rulfo returns from all the archipelagos

XII

RESERVADO

      lacónico
Quitado de bulla
Tímido
      sin delirio de grandeza
+ parecía monje taoísta
Que compatriota de Pedro Zamora

No se sabe qué es + admirable
Si el autor o la obra que dejó
Tanto vale la persona de Juan!
Un hombre como Rulfo
No podía hacer otra cosa
Que escribir esa biblia mexicana

Fuera de José María Arguedas
Y del inconmensurable cholo Vallejo
Pocos son los que pueden comparársele

XII

RESERVED

        laconic
Not noisy
Timid
        without delusions of grandeur
He resembled a Taoist monk
More than a countryman of Pedro Zamora

One doesn't know which is more admirable
The author or the work he left behind
Such a worthy person was Juan!
A man like Rulfo
Couldn't do anything other than
Write that Mexican bible

Outside of José María Arguedas
And Vallejo the incommensurable Indian
There are few can stand comparison with him

XIII

MENTIRÍA SI DIGO QUE ESTOY EMOCIONADO

Traumatizado es la palabra precisa
La noticia del premio
                    me dejó con la boca abierta
Dudo que pueda volver a cerrarla

XIII

I WOULD BE LYING IF I SAID I'M TOUCHED

The precise word is traumatized
News of the prize
                left me with my mouth wide open
I doubt that I can ever close it again

XIV

QUÉ SE HACE EN UN CASO COMO ÉSTE

x + que me pellizco no despierto
Me siento como alguien que se saca el gordo de la lotería
Sin haber comprado jamás un boleto
Sin compadres
                sin santos en la corte
No quedo en deuda con ninguna *maffia*
A sangre fría
                como debe ser
Alabado sea el Santísimo
Los *envidioses* que se vayan al diablo
Y a *nosotros* que me erijan un monumento
O no dicen ustedes...

XIV

WHAT DOES ONE DO IN A CASE LIKE THIS

No matter how much I pinch myself I don't wake up
I feel like someone who wins the lottery
Without ever having bought a ticket
Without cronies
                    without insider judges
I'm not beholden to any mafia
Serene
                    as should be
Praised be his Holiness
Let the *envious* go to hell
And to *us* let them erect me a monument
Or don't you think…

XV

ESPERABA ESTE PREMIO?

No
Los premios son
Como las Dulcineas del Toboso
Mientras + pensamos en ellas
+ lejanas
          + sordas
                    + enigmáticas

Los premios son para los espíritus libres
Y para los amigos del jurado

Chanfle
No contaban con mi astucia

XV

WAS I EXPECTING THIS PRIZE?

No
Prizes are
Like the Dulcineas of Toboso
The more we think about them
The further away
             the deafer
                      the more enigmatic

Prizes are for free spirits
And for friends of the jury

Curve ball
They didn't count on my sagacity*

*Translator's Note: Parra's use of the term "Chanfle" and the phrase "No
contaban con mi astucia" derive from a popular Mexican TV program
entitled *El Chapulín Colorado*, starring Mexican comedian Roberto Gómez
Bolaños as "The Red Grasshopper" (the meaning of the program title, with
"chapulín" a Nahuatl word). This spoof of superheroes was shown
throughout Latin America until 1979 but can still be seen as reruns.

XVI

VEN?

Alguien anda diciendo x ahí
Que el premiado no está a la altura del premio
Falta de cantidad y calidad
Hay x lo menos una docena
De candidatos muy superiores a él
Y yo le encuentro toda la razón*

Sé perfectamente
Que éste no es un premio para mí
Sino un homenaje a la poesía chilena
Y lo recibo con mucha humildad
En nombre de todos los poetas anónimos

*Arreola, Cardenal, etc., etc.

XVI

DO YOU SEE?

Somebody goes around here saying
That the winner doesn't come up to the prize
He lacks quantity and quality
There are at least a dozen
Candidates better than he is
And I totally agree*

I know perfectly well
That this award is not for me
But an homage to Chilean poetry
And I receive it with great humility
In the name of all the poets of anonymity

*Arreola, Cardenal, etc. etc.

XVII

UNA SOLA ADVERTENCIA

Si se trata de premiar el silencio
Como creo que éste es el caso
Nadie ha hecho + méritos que yo
Soy el menos prolífico de todos
Años de años que no publico nada

Me considero
Un drogadicto de la página en blanco
Como lo fuera el propio Juan Rulfo
Que se negó a escribir
+ de lo estrictamente necesario

XVII

A NOTE OF WARNING

If it's a matter of awarding silence
Which in this case I believe it is
No one has made himself more deserving
I'm the least prolific of all
Years and years of not publishing a thing

I consider myself
An addict of the blank page
As was the same Juan Rulfo
Who refused to write
Any more than was absolutely necessary

XVIII

QUÉ ME PROPONGO HACER CON TANTA PLATA?

Lo primero de todo la salud
En segundo lugar
Reconstruir la Torre de Marfil
Que se vino abajo con el terremoto

Ponerme al día con impuestos internos

Y una silla de ruedas x si las moscas...

XVIII

WHAT DO I PLAN TO SPEND SO MUCH MONEY ON?

First of all my health
In the second place
Rebuilding the Ivory Tower
Which came down with the earthquake

Catching up on my income taxes

And a wheelchair just in case...

XIX

LOS DETRACTORES DE LA POESÍA

Van a tener que pedirnos perdón en cuclillas
Ha quedado de manifiesto
Que se le puede hacer la pelea a la prosa:
La cenicienta de las bellas letras
No tiene nada que envidiar a sus hermanastras

Goza de buena salud
En opinión de justos y pecadores
Señores Fukuyama
                    Gombrowicz
                                Stendhal
Platón & Cía. Ilimitada

XIX

THOSE WHO SPEAK ILL OF POETRY

Will have to apologize on their hands and knees
It's been made clear
That prose can be taken on:
The Cinderella of belles lettres
Has nothing to envy in her stepsisters

She enjoys good health
In the opinion of the innocent and guilty
Misters Fukuyama
     Gombrowicz
       Stendhal
Plato & Co. Unlimited

XX

RULFO SE PUSO FIRME CONTRA VIENTO Y MAREA

Tres veces 100 y punto
                    ni una página +
El escritor no es una fábrica de cecinas

En lo que a mí respecta
17 años entre primer y segundo libro
Claro después pasó lo que pasó:
Se me moteja de poeta bisiesto
Paciencia
C/4 años un domingosiete
Plagios
          Adaptaciones
Gárgaras para combatir el insomnio
Ofrezco la palabra

XX

RULFO STOOD FIRM AGAINST ALL ODDS

Three times 100 and stop
                                not another page
The writer is not a sausage factory

With respect to myself
17 years between the first and second book
Well sure later came what came:
They call me the leap year poet
Patience
Every 4 years I'm pregnant again
Plagiarisms
        Adaptations
Garglings for fighting off insomnia
If anyone has something to say

XXI

PIDO LA PALABRA

Me llamo Pedro Páramo

No he leído a Juan Rulfo
Soy un hombre de campo
No tengo tiempo de leer a nadie

He oído decir eso sí
Que me deja muy mal en su novela

Sus razones tendrá digo yo
Nada en el mundo ocurre porque sí
Recordaráse que era un dipsómano compulsivo
Ojo
          nació en Sayula
Lugar de moscas en lengua mapuche
Él no tiene la culpa de nada

A ustedes probablemente sí
Pero a nosotros no nos mete el dedo en la boca don Juan

En lo que a mí se refiere
Soy un analfabeto compulsivo
No tengo ganas de leer a Pérez
(Ese era su nombre verdadero
Se lo cambió de un día para otro)
Yo leo sólo mis propios sonetos
Si les parece les recito uno
Que le escribí a la Susana San Juan
O será mejor que me multiplique x cero tal vez
Hacen mal en sacarme de la tumba!

XXI

LET ME PUT IN A WORD

My name is Pedro Páramo

I haven't read Juan Rulfo
I'm a man from the countryside
I don't have time for reading anyone

I have heard it said for sure
That in the novel he makes me come off very badly

I say that he will have his reasons
Nothing in the world happens on its own
Remember that he was a compulsive dipsomaniac
Watch out
                he was born in Sayula
A place of flies in the Mapuche tongue
He's not to blame for anything

He probably fooled you
But Don Juan doesn't pull the wool over our eyes

As for myself
I'm a compulsive illiterate
I don't have the least interest in reading Pérez
(That was his real name
He changed it from one day to the next)
I only read my own sonnets
If you like I'll recite one
Which I wrote to Susana San Juan
Or perhaps it would be better if I multiplied by zero
You were wrong to drag me out of my grave!

XXII

PARALELO CON HAMLET

Hay fantasmas y espectros en ambos casos
En ambos casos corre mucha sangre
Sí señor
Hijos que se rebelan contra sus progenitores
Etc., etc.,
Personaje difuso
Con + trazas de Hamlet que de Telémaco me parece a mí
Claro que con una diferencia x lo muy menos
Juan Preciado no tiene mucho de príncipe
Cristiano vulgar y silvestre
Peor aún
Hijo legítimo pero sólo
Desde un punto de vista burocrático
+ mendigo que rey
Llega a Comala a pie
                              sin equipaje
Con la orden expresa de vengar a su padre
CÓBRASELO CARO HIJO MÍO
Pedro Páramo debe morir
Aunque no x delitos isabelinos
Ojo
x ofensas de orden económico...
No se trata de un viaje de placer

XXII

PARALLEL WITH HAMLET

There are ghosts and spirits in both
In each case a lot of bloodletting
Yes sir
Sons who rebel against their progenitors
Etc., etc.,
A wide-ranging character
With it seems to me more traces of Hamlet than Telemachus
Of course with at least a small difference
Juan Preciado isn't much of a prince
An average Christian
Even worse
A legitimate son but only
From a bureaucratic point of view
More a beggar than a king
Arrives in Comala on foot
                              without a suitcase
With the express order to take revenge on his daddy
MAKE HIM PAY DEARLY MY SON
Pedro Páramo must die
Though not for Elizabethan crimes
Notice
For offenses of a monetary kind...
It's not about a pleasure trip

XXIII

VEO QUE SE ME ESTÁN QUEDANDO DORMIDOS

Ésa es la idea
Yo parto de la base
De que el discurso debe ser aburrido
Mientras + soporífero mejor
De lo contrario nadie aplaudiría
Y el orador será tildado de pícaro

XXIII

I SEE THAT YOU'RE ABOUT TO FALL ASLEEP

That's the idea
I work on the theory
That the speech should be boring
The more soporific the better
Otherwise no one would applaud
And the speaker'd be considered a rogue

XXIV

EL ESPAÑOL ES UNA LENGUA MUERTA

Moribunda en el mejor de los quesos
Es x eso que Rulfo redactó su Quijote
En el habla del siglo XVI

XXIV

SPANISH IS A DEAD LANGUAGE

Moribund in the best of cheesy cases
It's for that reason that Rulfo couched his Quijote
In sixteenth-century speech

XXV

POR EVITAR LA TRAMPA DEL VERSO

Los escritores suelen caer en la prosa
Que es un vicio tan tonto como el otro
Cosa que no ocurre con Rulfo

No se diga que Rulfo escribe en prosa

XXV

TO AVOID THE VERSE TRAP

Writers tend to fall into prose
That's a vice as dumb as the other
Something that doesn't happen with Rulfo

No one says that Rulfo writes in prose

XXVI

RULFO TIENE SOBRE LOS POETAS CONVENCIONALES

Incluidos los antipoetas
La ventaja
De no escribir jamás en verso

Ni siquiera en el verso llamado libre
Que es el + artificioso de todos
Según un gato llamado Ezra Pound

El que no se menea es vaca
Claro
                    porque la gente no habla en verso
No sé si me explico
Lo que quiero decir es otra cosa

XXVI

RULFO HAS OVER CONVENTIONAL POETS

Including antipoets
The advantage
Of never writing in verse

Not even in so-called free verse
Which is the most artificial of all
According to a cat named Ezra Pound

He who doesn't fidget is an idiot
Sure
          because people don't speak in verse
I don't know if I make myself clear
What I want to say is something else

XXVII

LA REPÚBLICA *HIDEAL* DEL FUTURO

Suprimirá los premios literarios
Pues no somos caballos de carrera
x un deudor feliz
Cuántos acreedores postergados…

XXVII

THE FUTURE *HIDEAL* REPUBLIC

Will suppress all literary prizes
Since we are not race horses
For one happy debtor
How many deserving passed over...

XXVIII

RULFO LE DA LA RAZÓN A HEIDEGGER

Es fundación del ser x la palabra
Es un lenguaje que deviene opaco
(Jakobson)
Es un enigma que se niega a ser descifrado x los profesores

Y también le da la razón a Machado

Qué es *Pedro Páramo*?
Qué es *El llano en llamas*?

Unas pocas palabras verdaderas!

XXVIII

RULFO THINKS HEIDEGGER IS RIGHT

Being is founded on the word
It's a language that becomes opaque
(Jakobson)
It's an enigma the professors cannot decipher

And he also thinks Machado is right

What is *Pedro Páramo?*
What is *The Plain in Flames?*

A few truthful words!

XXIX

AL PASO QUE VA RULFO

Terminará sentándose en el piano
Yo diría que ya se nos sentó
Nos vendió pan a todos x parejo
De sacristán a fraile

Comparados con Rulfo
Nuestros escritores parecen volantines de plomo
No queda + que sacarle el sombrero

Lo que es yo me declaro
Rulfiólogo de jornada completa

Mucho cuidado sí
Con confundir rulfiólogo con rulfista
Rulfista con rulfiano
Rulfiano con rulfófilo
Rulfófilo con rulfómano
Rulfómano con rulfópata
Rulfópata con rulfófobo
Sí:
Se ruega no confundir rulfófobo con rulfófago

XXIX

AT THE RATE RULFO IS GOING

He'll end up at the top of the heap
I would say he's already left us far behind
He sold bread equally to everyone
From sexton to monk

Compared with Rulfo
Our writers are like kites of lead
To him we can only take off our hats

As for me I declare myself
A full-time Rulfologue

But be very careful
Not to confuse Rulfologue with Rulfist
Rulfist with Rulfian
Rulfian with Rulfophile
Rulfophile with Rulfomaniac
Rulfomaniac with Rulfopath
Rulfopath with Rulfophobe
Yes:
Please don't confuse Rulfophobe with Rulfophage

XXX

HIPERREALISMO TESTIMONIAL

Hay que colgarle una etiqueta a ese Rulfo
Páginas en blanco
La fundación del ser x el silencio

Corrupción en las altas y en las bajas esferas
Sacerdotes armados hasta los dientes
Andan que se las pelan x el paisaje
Pancho Villa a la vista
Lo que oyen señoras y señores
Una pobre mujer
Agujereada x su propio padre
Pide silencio desde el lecho de muerte:
Justina
          hazme el favor de irte a llorar a otra parte

XXX

HYPERREALISM TESTIMONIAL

We have to pin a label on that Rulfo
Blank pages
The state of being founded on silence

Corruption in high and low places
Priests armed to the teeth
Darting over the landscape
Pancho Villa in sight
What you hear ladies and gentlemen
Is a poor woman
Violated by her own father
Begging for a little quiet on her deathbed:
Justina
            do me a favor and go sob somewhere else

XXXI

DISCURSO DE GUADALAJARA

afonía total
Huelo + a cipreses que a laureles

XXXI

GUADALAJARA SPEECH

    complete loss of my voice
I smell more like cypresses than laurels

XXII

CERO PROBLEMA

Con este premio paso a la categoría
De caballero de la triste figura:

Donde me siente yo
Está la cabecera de la mesa caramba!

+ información
En soneto que está x publicarse

No sé si me explico
Lo que quiero decir es viva Chile
Viva la Confederación Perú-boliviana

XXXII

NOT A PROBLEM

With this prize I move into the category
Of the knight of the woeful figure:

Wherever I sit down
Damned if it's not the head of the table!

More information
In my sonnet that's about to be published

I don't know if I make myself clear
What I want to say is Long Live Chile
Long Live the Peruvian-Bolivian Confederacy

XXXIII

APOYO LA IDEA GENIAL

           de Ricardo Serrano
Que propone elevar al triple
El monto del Premio Juan Rulfo
De Literatura Iberoamericana

A condición eso sí
De que sea con efecto retroactivo

XXXIII

I SUPPORT THE INGENIOUS IDEA

of Ricardo Serrano
Who proposes to triple
The amount of the Juan Rulfo Prize
Of Iberoamerican Literature

On the condition of course
That it be applied retroactively

XXXIV

DESPUÉS DEL RULFO SUEÑA CON EL NOBEL?

Me pregunta al oído una prostituta
Como si yo fuera la Susana San Juan
Y ella el padre Rentería

Y yo le respondo con otra pregunta:

Si no se lo dieron a Rulfo
Por qué me lo van a dar a mí?

XXXIV

AFTER THE RULFO DO YOU DREAM OF THE NOBEL?

A whore whispers in my ear
As if I were Susana San Juan
And she Father Rentería

And I reply with another question:

If they didn't give it to Rulfo
Why would they give it to me?

XXXV

CUÁL ES LA MORALEJA

de este cuento:
Que parece estar alargándose + de la cuenta
Muy sencillo señoras y señores
Hay que volver a releer a Rulfo
Yo no lo conocía créanmelo
Me encantaba
pero eso era todo
No lo había leído en profundidad
Ahora veo cómo son las cosas
Agradezco los narco-dólares
Harta falta que me venían haciendo
Pero mi gran trofeo es Pedro Páramo
No sé qué decir
A los 77 años de edad
He visto la luz
+ que la luz he visto las tinieblas

XXXV

WHAT IS THE MORAL

                        of this story:
Which seems to be getting longer & longer
Very simple ladies and gentlemen
We must reread Rulfo again
I never knew him believe me
He delighted me
                        but that's all
I had not read him closely
Now I see the way things are
I appreciate the narco-dollars
I have sure been needing them
But my great trophy is Pedro Páramo
I don't know what to say
At 77 years of age
I have seen the light
More than the light I have seen the darkness

XXXVI

DE ACUERDO

Alle Kultur nach Auschwitz ist Müll
Traduzco
Toda la cultura posterior a Auschwitz
Es
          basura
Digamos...casi toda señor Adorno

XXXVI

IN AGREEMENT

Alle Kultur nach Auschwitz ist Müll
I translate
All culture after Auschwitz
Is...
        garbage
Let's say...almost all Mr. Adorno

XXXVII

FRASES PA(R)RA EL BRONCE

1

Porvenir
Una bomba de tiempo

2

Consumismo
                    serpiente
Que se traga a sí misma x la cola

3

Mucho se habla de derechos humanos
Poco
            nada casi de deberes humanos
Primer deber humano
Respetar los derechos humanos

4

Vuelta a la democracia para qué
Para que se repita la película?
NO:
Para ver si podemos salvar el planeta
Sin democracia no se salva nada

5

Tercer y último llamado
Individualistas del mundo uníos
Antes que sea demasiado tarde

XXXVII

PAR(R)APHRASES TO BE ENGRAVED IN BRONZE

1

The future
A time bomb

2

Consumerism
          a snake
That swallows its tail

3

A lot of talk about human rights
Little
      almost nothing about human responsibilities
Number one human responsibility
To respect human rights

4

Return to democracy for what
To see the same film over again?
NO:
To see if we can save the planet
Without democracy nothing is saved

5

Third and final call
Individualists of the world unite
Before it's way too late

XXXVIII

SEGÚN DON ALFONSO REYES

La diferencia entre hombre y mujer
Está en la ortografía
La mujer tiene mala ortografía
Según don Alfonso
Qué dirá Derridá de todo esto?
Vive la différance
                              qué duda cabe
Pero qué es la diferencia para él?
La huella!
Y qué es la huella?
La huella derridiana no es:
No es nada
Y no puede encasillarse
En la pregunta metafísica "qué es?"

La huella
Sencilla y completamente
Es la huella de la huella
La huella no es perceptible ni imperceptible
La huella es el devenir-espacio del tiempo
Y el devenir-tiempo del espacio

¿Capisco?

XXXVIII

ACCORDING TO DON ALFONSO REYES

The difference between man and woman
Is in their spelling
According to Don Alfonso
Woman is a bad speller
What would Derrida say of all this?
Vive la différance
                    no doubt*
But to him what is the difference?
The trace!
But what is the trace?
The Derridean trace is not:
It's nothing
It can't be classified
In the metaphysical question "what is?"

The trace
Simply and completely
Is the print of the trace
The trace is neither perceptible nor imperceptible
The trace is the becoming-space of time
And the becoming-time of space

Capisco?

---

*Translator's note: Parra is alluding here and later in the poem to Jacques Derrida's deconstructionist theory that the idea of *différance* brings with it the idea of "trace," that is, what a sign differs or defers from, and that the trace does not exist because it is self-effacing.

XXXIX

SILENCIO MIERDA

Con 2000 años de mentira basta!

XXXIX

SILENCE SHITHEAD

2000 years of lying is enough!

XL

LA MUJER

Hay un punto
Que no podemos dejar de tocar
En ocasión tan álgida como ésta
Voy a cederle la palabra a un muchacho
Que en pleno siglo XIX
Sabía ya lo que estaba diciendo
Comillas:
Cuando se rompan las cadenas que esclavizan a la mujer
Cuando ella pueda vivir por sí misma y para sí misma
Cuando el hombre
                    sujeto abominable hasta aquí
La haya liberado
La mujer también accederá a lo desconocido

Sus constelaciones de ideas diferirán de las nuestras?
Ella hallará también cosas extrañas
Insondables
                    horribles
                                    deliciosas
Que nosotros sabremos apreciar
Que nosotros sabremos comprender

(Rimbaud, *Carta del vidente*)

XL

WOMAN

There's one point
That we can't leave out
On an occasion as chilly as this
I'm going to yield the floor to a boy
Who in the middle of the XIXth century
Even then knew what he was talking about
In quotes:
When the chains enslaving woman are broken
When she can live on her own and for herself
When man
              up to now an abominable subject
Has freed her
Woman too will approach the unknown

Will her constellations of ideas differ from our own?
She too will discover the strangest things
Inscrutable
              horrible
                        delicious
Which we will know how to appreciate
Which we will know how to comprehend

(Rimbaud, *The Prophet's Letter*)

XLI

BIEN

El sol miró para atrás
Ésa es la verdad de las cosas
Se demostró que 2 + 2 son 4
O algo x el estilo
Sursum corda
Ahora sí que se fue la bolita

+ vale tarde que nunca
Habría dicho Violeta Parra

Hasta que llovió en Sayula señor rector

Ahora sí que seremos felices
Ahora sí que podremos cantar
Aquella canción que dice así
Con su ritmo tropical

XLI

OKAY

The sun emerged from the clouds
That's the truth of the matter
It was demonstrated that 2 + 2 are 4
Or something like that
Lift up your hearts
That's the way things are

Better late than never
Violeta Parra would've said

It even rained in Sayula Mr. Rector

Yes now we will be happy
Yes now we will be able to sing
That song that says it this way
With its tropical rhythm

XLII

EN RESUMEN

en síntesis
En buen romance
voto x Rulfo
Decididamente que me quedo con Rulfo

Cómo que por qué
Por haber llevado a la práctica
Las instrucciones de González Martínez
Su compatriota de Guadalajara
Qué instrucciones son ésas?

Punto uno:
    tuércele el cuello al cisne de engañoso plumaje
    que da su nota blanca al azul de la fuente
    él pasea su gracia no más, pero no siente
    el alma de las cosas ni la voz del paisaje

Punto dos:
    huye de toda forma y de todo lenguaje
    que no vayan acordes con el ritmo latente
    de la vida profunda ... y adora intensamente
    la vida, y que la vida comprenda tu homenaje

Y punto final:
    mira al sapiente búho cómo tiende las alas
    desde el Olimpo, deja el regazo de Palas
    y posa en aquel árbol el vuelo taciturno...

    él no tiene la gracia del cisne, mas su inquieta
    pupila que se clava en la sombra, interpreta
    el misterioso libro del silencio nocturno

XLII

IN SHORT

      to sum up
In plain talk
          I vote for Rulfo
I will decidedly stick with Rulfo

What do you mean why
For having put into practice
The instructions of González Martínez
His compatriot from Guadalajara
What instructions are those?

Point one:
      wring the neck of the swan whose deceptive plumage
      reflects its white note upon the blue-water fountain
      he only shows off his gracefulness but never sounds
      the soul of things nor the voice of the landscape

Point two:
      Flee from every form and every language
      that does not accord with the latent rhythm
      of a deep-felt life ... and lend intense adoration
      to life, and may life understand your homage

And final point:
      watch the wise owl how he spreads his wings
      from Olympus, leaves the lap of Pallas
      and in that tree alights his taciturn flight...

      he hasn't the grace of the swan, but his restless
      eye in piercing the darkness is interpreting
      the mysterious pages of noiseless night

XLIII

REPETIRÉ QUE ME PRONUNCIO POR RULFO

Los demás me parecen excelentes
Pero no me enloquecen en absoluto

Mientras los compañeros
Se dedicaban a enjaular a los pájaros libertarios
Él iba de un lado a otro
Resucitando muertos y vivos
Y a mí me encanta hacer estornudar a la gente

Si yo fuera el autor de *La tercera orilla del río*
Me atrevería a decir
Que me considero su hermano gemelo

XLIII

I'LL REPEAT THAT I'M ALL FOR RULFO

To me the others seem excellent
But I'm not nuts about any of them

While his friends
Were busy caging up the anarchist birds
He was going from place to place
Resuscitating the dead and alive
As for me I love to make people sneeze

If I were the author of *The Third Bank of the River*
I would dare to say
That I consider myself his twin brother

XLIV

PERDONE SEÑOR PARRA

Si admira tanto a Rulfo
Por qué no se escribe una novela?

Porque como su nombre lo indica
La novela no-ve-la realidad
Salvo que sea Rulfo quien la escriba

Qué opinión le merece
El colapso ecológico del planeta?

No veo para qué tanta alharaca
Ya sabemos que el mundo se acabó

¿Culpables?

El lingam y la yoni
Ver explosión demográfica

Miserere di me...
El error consistió
En creer que la tierra era nuestra
Cuando la verdad de las cosas
Es que nosotros
         somos
                  de
                       la
                            tierra
No sé
El respetable público dirá

XLIV

PARDON ME MR. PARRA

If you admire Rulfo so much
Why don't you write a novel?

Because as its name in Spanish indicates
The *novela* no-see-the reality
Except if it's Rulfo who's writing it

What view do you take
Of the planet's ecological collapse?

I don't see what all the fuss is about
We know the world ended long ago

Who's to blame?

The lingam and yoni
Note the demographic explosion

Have mercy on me...
The error consisted
In believing the earth was ours
When the truth of the matter is
That we
       belong
           to
               the
                  earth
I don't know
The audience will say

XLV

ULTIMATUM

O redactan de una vez x todas
La encíclica de la supervivencia carajo
O voy a tener que redactarla yo mismo
Solloza a voz en cuello
vuestro señor Jesucristo
De Elqui
Domingo Zárate Vega
Alias *el ecóloco* del norte chico
Hurry up!
Eternidades hay pero no muchas

El planeta ya no da para +

XLV

ULTIMATUM

Either they draw up once and for all
The encyclical letter on survival
Or I'll have to put it in writing myself
Weeps at the top of his voice
Your Lord Jesus Christ
Of Elqui
Domingo Zárate Vega
Alias the *eco loco* of the north
Hurry up!
There are eternities but not so many

The planet can't take it any more

XLVI

TERMINARÉ X DONDE DEBÍ COMENZAR

Ni socialista ni capitalista
Sino todo lo contrario:
                Ecologista
Propuesta de Daimiel:
Entendemos x ecologismo
Un movimiento socioeconómico
Basado en la idea de armonía
De la especie humana con su medio
Que lucha x una vida lúdica
Creativa
        igualitaria
             pluralista
Libre de explotación
Y basada en la comunicación
Y colaboración de las personas
A continuación vienen los 12 puntos

XLVI

I WILL END WHERE I SHOULD HAVE BEGUN

Neither socialist nor capitalist
Totally the opposite:
                    Ecologist
Daimiel's proposal:
We understand by ecologism
A socio-economic movement
Based on the idea of harmony
Between the human species and its environment
Of fighting for a happy life
Creative
              egalitarian
                        pluralist
Free of exploitation
And founded on the communication
And cooperation of all persons
Immediately following is the 12-point plan

XLVII

GRACIAS SEÑORES MIEMBROS DEL JURADO

Por este premio tan inmerecido
José Luis Martínez y Ramón Xirau de México
Claude Fell de Francia
Bella Joszef de Brasil
Julio Ortega del Perú
Ángel Flores de Puerto Rico
John Brushwood de los EUA
Carlos Bousoño de España
Fernando Alegría de Chile

XLVII

THANK YOU GENTLEMEN MEMBERS OF THE JURY

For this prize so undeserved
José Luis Martínez and Ramón Xirau of Mexico
Claude Fell of France
Bella Joszef of Brazil
Julio Ortega of Peru
Ángel Flores of Puerto Rico
John Brushwood of the U.S.A.
Carlos Bousoño of Spain
Fernando Alegría of Chile

XLVIII

MIS AGRADECIMIENTOS + SINCEROS

Al gobierno del estado de Jalisco
Al ayuntamiento de Guadalajara
Al Fondo de Cultura Económica
A PEMEX a PIPSA a BANAMEX a BANCOMER
Y muy muy en particular
A la Lotería Nacional para la Asistencia Pública
Sin lotería yo no estoy aquí
Se comprueba la teoría de Leonardo:
1 % de inspiración
2 de transpiración
Y el resto suerte

XLVIII

MY MOST SINCERE GRATITUDE

To the government of the state of Jalisco
To the city council of Guadalajara
To the Cultural Economic Press
To PEMEX to PIPSA to BANAMEX to BANCOMER
And very very especially
To the National Lottery for Public Assistance
If it weren't for the lottery I wouldn't be here
It proves Leonardo's theory:
1% inspiration
2 of perspiration
And the rest pure luck

XLIX

A QUIÉN DEDICAR ESTE PREMIO?

Respondo sin pensarlo dos veces
A Dios señor rector
Exista o no exista
Gracias
Es un honor muy grande para mí
Me despido con un abrazo bien apretado
Y con la autoridad irrestricta
Que le confiere el águila a la serpiente
Música maestro!
Doy x finiquitado el siglo XX
Good bye to all that
Hasta cuándo señoras y señores
In nomine Patri
        et Filii
              et Spiritus Sancti
Doy x inaugurado el siglo XXI
Fin a la siutiquería grecolatinizante
Venga el bu
No + mentiras piadosas
Hay que decirle la verdad al lector
Aunque se le pongan los pelos de punta
Basta de subterfugios
Asumamos de una vez x todas
Nuestra precariedad agropecuaria
Lo demás es literatura
Mala literatura modernista

A otro Parra con ese hueso Señor Rector

XLIX

TO WHOM DO I DEDICATE THIS PRIZE?

I answer without giving it a second thought
To God Mr. Rector
Whether he exists or not
Thanks
It's a great honor for me
I bid you farewell with a firm embrace
And with the unlimited authority
That the eagle confers on the serpent
Music maestro!
I give you at the conclusion of the XXth century
Good bye to all that
Until whenever ladies and gentlemen
In the name of the Father
    and of the Son
        and of the Holy Ghost
I give you at the beginning of the XXIst century
The quietus to the Greco-Latin farce
Let the bogey man come
No more pious lies
One has to tell the reader the truth
Even if his hairs should stand on end
Enough of subterfuge
Let's accept once and for all
Our land and cattle precariousness
The rest is literature
Bad modernist literature

Toss another Parra that bone Mr. Rector

A mí me carga la literatura
Tanto o + que la antiliteratura

Si tuviera 20 años me iría al África
A comerciar en estupefacientes

Guadalajara
A 23 de noviembre de 1991

I detest literature
As much as or more than antiliterature

If I were 20 I would go to Africa
And traffic in stupefying drugs

Guadalajara
November 23, 1991

L

ÚLTIMA HORA-URGENTE

Ayer conocí en el café Nápoles
A un muchacho que lee mucho
Tiene capacidad para hacer hablar a los muertos
Y escribe sapo con zeta
Se firma Juan Rulfo
Pero su verdadero nombre es Juan Pérez
Troika
Han pasado los años
Hoy todo el mundo sabe quién es Rulfo
Se le compara con el propio Cervantes
Y yo propongo que en lo sucesivo
La palabra sapo se escriba con zeta

En honor a este huaso mexicano

MAI MAI PEÑI*

*Saludo mapuche, algo así como "hola hermano".

L

FLASH – BREAKING NEWS

Yesterday I met in the Naples café
A boy who reads a lot
He has the capacity to make dead people talk
And writes frog with ph
He signs himself Juan Rulfo
But his real name is Juan Pérez
Troika
The years have come and gone
Nowadays everyone knows who Rulfo is
He's even compared with Cervantes himself
And I propose that in the future
The word frog be spelled with ph

In honor of this Mexican huaso

MAI MAI PEÑI*

*Mapuche greeting, something like "hello brother."
Translator's note: Huaso is a Chilean cowboy.

HAPPY BIRTHDAY

I

QUISIERA AGRADECER

A los organizadores de este encuentro
La oportunidad que se me da
A mí que soy el + sospechoso de los invitados
Para saludar a todos los presentes
En especial a los apóstoles del Teatro de las Naciones
Reunidos por primera vez en Mapocho
Que es el verdadero nombre de Santiago de Chile*
Lejos lejos del mundanal ruido
Como decíamos anteayer

Es que todavía confiamos en algo parece
Plenamente conscientes eso sí
De la precariedad de nuestros medios
Nos se diga que somos unos payasos irresponsables

*Videlicit el nombre que tenía
  A la llegada de los invasores

HAPPY BIRTHDAY

I

I WOULD LIKE TO THANK

The organizers of this gathering
For the opportunity it gives to me
Who is the most suspect of all the guests
To greet the present company
Especially the apostles of the Theater of Nations
Reunited for the first time in Mapocho
Which is the true name of Santiago Chile*
Far far from the mundane noise
As we were saying two days ago

It seems that we still believe in something
Fully aware that is
Of our imperiled resources
Not to be called a bunch of irresponsible clowns

*Videlicet the name it had
  When the invaders arrived

113

II

ALGO HUELE MUY MAL EN DINAMARCA lo sé

Ya cruzamos el umbral del Apocalipsis
Aseguran los + pesimistas
El problema no tiene solución
Es de mal tono hablar de estas cosas
El smog
      el ozono
            el consumismo suiSIDA
Lo sentimos muchísimo
No depende de nuestra voluntad
El teatro del mundo se acaba
Nos hundimos irremisiblemente en la nada
¿Con la bandera al tope?
              tanto peor!
Aquí no se respeta ni la ley de la selva

II

SOMETHING IN DENMARK SMELLS REAL BAD I know

We have already crossed the threshold of the Apocalypse
We're assured by the most pessimistic
The problem has no solution
It's uncouth to speak of such things
Smog
         ozone
                   consumerism HIVicide
We regret it greatly
It's not up to us
The theater of the world is done for
We have sunk ourselves hopelessly into nothingness
With the flag flying high?
                              so much the worse
Here not even the law of the jungle gets any respect

III

EXPLOSIÓN DEMOGRÁFICA

culpables
El lingam & la yoni*

sí señor:
Extirpación del Miembro Viril
Es lo que corresponde en estos casos

*Genitales en sánscrito

III

POPULATION EXPLOSION

the culprits are
The lingam & yoni*

yes sir:
Cutting off the Virile Member
Is in such a case the only answer

*Genitals in Sanskrit

IV

HORROR DE HORRORES

Lo único que nos está permitido
Es
La comercialización de la catástrofe

Exageran los amigos catastrofistas...
¿Y si llegaran a tener razón?

No sé
Del otro lado están los optimistas:
Dios proveerá
Hay que confiar en Él y en el Demonio
Teletón 93
Hay tanto x hacer...

IV

HORROR OF HORRORS

The only thing we're permitted
Is
The commercialization of the catastrophe

Our friends the catastrophists exaggerate...
And if it turns out they're right?

I don't know
On the other side are the optimists:
God will provide
One has to trust in Him and in the Devil
Telethon for Disabled Children 93
There's so much left to do...

V

TAMBIÉN ESTÁN LOS PÍCAROS

Disfrazados de padre de la patria
No se preocupen
           no se preocupen
El asilo de ancianos tomará cartas en el asunto
Conversen con el alcalde
Es un señor de buenas intenciones

Y mientras tanto vamos echando
400 vehículos + a la calle cada día
Vamos exterminando el mar
           el bosque nativo

Los japoneses tienen la palabra

V

THERE ARE ALSO THE RASCALS

Disguised as a Founding Father
Don't be concerned
                              don't be concerned
The home for the elderly poor will take up the matter
Speak with the mayor
He's a man with good intentions

And in the meantime we go on loosing
400 more vehicles on the streets every day
Go on exterminating the sea
                              the native woods

The Japanese have the floor

VI

ENTENDEMOS X ECOLOGISMO

Dicen las minorías españolas
Un movimiento socioeconómico
Basado en la idea de armonía
            de la especie humana con su medio
Que lucha por una vida lúdica
                            creativa
                                    igualitaria
                                        pluralista
Libre de explotación

Y basada en la comunicación
Y colaboración de grandes & chicos

A continuación
Vienen los 12 puntos:

VI

WE UNDERSTAND BY ECOLOGISM

Say the Spanish minorities
A socioeconomic movement
Based on the idea of harmony
            between the human species and its environment
Which fights for a life of pastime
                                    creativity
                                            equality
                                                    pluralism

Free of exploitation

And based on communication
And collaboration of big & little guys

Right afterwards
Come the 12 points:

VII

ALÓ!

      con quién hablo?…

Con un enfermo de la duda metódica
Hamlet
      Príncipe de Dinamarca a la orden
El Espectro me dice que actúe
Para vengar la muerte de mi madre
Perdón:
Para vengar la muerte de mi padre
Pero yo no estoy seguro de nada
Soy un cero a la izquierda lo reconozco
No sé si pegarme un tiro
O continuar viviendo x inercia

VII

HELLO!

with whom am I speaking?…

With one ill with methodical doubt
Hamlet
Prince of Denmark at your command
The Ghost tells me that I should act
To take revenge for my mother's death
Pardon me:
To take revenge for my father's death
But I'm not certain of anything
I do know I'm a zero to the left
I can't tell whether to shoot myself
Or live on through inertia

VIII

W.C. PrOblEM

To P or not to P
> That is the question

Agrupación de Enfermos a la Próstata

Qué será preferible me pregunto
Soportar los caprichos del destino funesto
O rebelarse contra ese mar de tribulaciones
& terminar con ellas para siempre

Morir
> dormir
>> no más

Y por así decirlo con un sueño
Poner fin a las cuitas del corazón
Y a los miles de riesgos naturales
A que se expone la mísera carne
La tentación no puede ser mayor

Morir...
> dormir...
>> ¿dormir?: tal vez soñar...

Ah! ahí está la clave
Puesto que en ese sueño de la muerte
Lo que pudiera ser de nuestros sueños
Una vez sacudida la mortal envoltura
Nos detiene la mano
> lo que explica
Que esta miseria no termine nunca

VIII

W.C. PrOblEM

To P or not to P
          That is the question

Association of Prostate Patients

Which would be preferable I ask myself
Suffer the whims of unfortunate fate
Or take arms against a sea of troubles
& by opposing end them

To die
          to sleep
                    no more
And by a sleep to say
We end the heartaches
And the thousand natural shocks
That flesh is heir to
The temptation couldn't be greater

To die...
          to sleep...
                    to sleep? perhaps to dream...
Ay, there's the rub
For in that sleep of death
What dreams may come
When we have shuffl'd off this mortal coil
Must give us pause
                    which explains
Why this misery will never end

Quién estaría dispuesto a seguir sufriendo
Las arbitrariedades del tirano
La burocracia de la justicia
Los latigazos y la burla del tiempo
Las convulsiones del amor despreciado
Las insolencias de la fuerza bruta
Los achaques de la vejez
Y los desdenes que el trabajo honrado
Recibe siempre de parte del cínico
Cuando yo mismo puedo cancelarme
Con una daga vulgar & silvestre

Por qué sudando y refunfuñando
Bajo la carga de una vida abyecta
Sólo porque el temor a la incógnita del más allá
Ignorado país de donde nunca
Ningún viajero regresó jamás
Inmoviliza al espíritu
Y nos obliga a seguir vegetando en este valle de lágrimas
En vez de emigrar a otros desconocidos
Así es como la conciencia hace realmente de nosotros
Unos cobardes
Así es como el matiz original de una resolución
Es empañado por el tinte pálido del pensamiento
El pensamiento paraliza la voluntad
Y hasta los compromisos más solemnes
Mueren en el instante de nacer

Ahí viene la bella Ophelia
                                    Silencio…
Ninfa
        ahora y en la hora
Ruega por este mísero pecador

Who would be disposed to put up with
The tyrant's outrages
The law's bureaucratic delays
The whips and scorns of time
The pangs of dispriz'd love
The insolence of brutal force
The infirmities of age
The disdain that honorable labor
Ever receives in the name of the cynic
When I myself can make my own quietus
With a rude & rustic knife

Why continue sweating & muttering
Under an abject life
Just from fear of the unknown land
Undiscover'd country from whose bourn
No traveler returns
It immobilizes the will
And makes us go on vegetating in this vale of tears
Instead of emigrating to others we know not of
Thus conscience does make
Cowards of us all
And thus the native hue of resolution
Is sicklied o'er with the pale cast of thought
Thought paralyzes will
And even the most solemn commitments
Die even as they're about to be born

Here comes the beautiful Ophelia
                              Soft you now...
Nymph
        in every hour of your orisons
Pray for this miserable sinner

IX

A VER A VER

Para qué se hizo el tiempo muchacho

Para que los acontecimientos
No ocurran todos de una vez

Correcto concursante nº 17!…

Por qué te dedicas a la poesía?

Porque no le tengo miedo al rid~~ípoto~~culo

A quién piensas dedicar tus Obras Completas

A Dios
        exista o no exista

Políticamente
Cómo te defines en la actualidad

Como un anarquista renovado

Vuelta a la democracia para qué!
Para que se repita la película?

Nóóó…
Para ver si podemos salvar el planeta:
Sin democracia no se salva nada

IX

LET'S SEE LET'S SEE

For what was time made young man

So events don't happen
All at once

Correct contestant number 17!...

Why do you dedicate yourself to poetry

Because I'm not afraid of the reardiculous

To whom will you dedicate your Complete Works

To God
        existent or not

Politically
How at present do you define yourself

As a reborn anarchist

Return to democracy for what!
To have the same movie shown again?

Noooo...
To see if we can save the planet:
Without democracy nothing is saved

Qué nota le pondrías
Al Primer Mandatario de la Nación
Aquí presente
                    (silencio prolongado)

Un seis a siete…
En escala de 1 a 5

Creo que ha hecho todo … o casi todo
Lo que la realidad objetiva permite

What grade would you give
To the Head of Our Nation
Here with us today
                    (prolonged silence)

A six or a seven
On a scale of 1 to 5

I believe he has done all ... or almost all
That objective reality allows

X

Y PARA COMENZAR A TERMINAR

Quién es Pablo Neruda para ti

Uno de los poetas + grandes del siglo XX

Cómo te relacionas con él

A little more than kin and less than kind

Algo + que parientes lejanos
Pero bastante menos que hermanos siameses

X

AND TO BEGIN TO END

Who to you is Pablo Neruda

One of the greatest poets of the twentieth century

How do you relate yourself to him

A little more than kin and less than kind

Something more than distant relations
But not nearly so close as Siamese twins

XI

Y AHORA VIENE UN AUTO SACRAMENTAL
O comercial o como quiera llamársele:

Su Santidad! Su Santidad!

Qué pasa…

Présteme 5000 pesos
mientras que me enderezo

Cómo no pues hijo
Con mucho gusto

Sea bueno Su Santidad
Y páseme 10 en vez de 5

Ahí tienes hijo…

Gracias Su Santidad
                    Dios se lo pague
¿Me podría prestar el Papamóvil
Para ir a dar una vuelticita?…

Mais ouis mais alors
                    es tuyo
                              te lo regalo
Que te vaya bien hijo mío

Se pasó Su Santidad!

XI

AND NOW COMES A SACRAMENTAL AUTO
Or commercial or whatever you want to call it:

Your Holiness! Your Holiness!

What is it...

Loan me 5000 pesos
Until I can get myself together

Why not son
I'd be happy to

Be a pal Your Holiness
Let me have 10 instead of 5

There you are son...

Thanks Your Holiness
                May God repay you
Would you loan me your Popemobile
For taking a little spin?...

Why sure thing
                it's yours
                                my gift to you
Have a good time my son

Your Holiness you outdid yourself!

XII

PAPAMÓVIL

La nueva marca de autos

- el vehículo del siglo XXI*

- confort y seguridad
  al alcance de todos los bolsillos

- sin fines de lucro

- cómodas cuotas mensuales

- un sueño hecho realidad
  gracias
  a la magnanimidad del Sumo Pontífice

*el vehípoto del siglo XXI

XII

POPEMOBILE

The new brand of cars

- the vehicle of the 21st century*

- comfort and safety
  within reach of every pocketbook

- not for profit

- easy monthly installments

- a dream come true
  thanks
  to the magnanimity of the Sovereign Pontiff

*the vasshicle of the 21st century

XIII

HABLA EL MINISTRO DEL RAMO

No nos hacemos eco
De comentarios malintencionados:
Hasta un niño de pecho sabe
Que la lombriz solitaria de la extrema pobreza
Viene de los gobiernos anteriores

Reconocemos que el índice de desocupación
Es algo + alto de lo deseable
Pero nos hacemos un deber en recordar
Que la Moneda no es una agencia de empleos

Camas no faltan en los hospitales
Lo que sucede es que sobran enfermos…
Hay un número exagerado de enfermos en este país
La verdad de los hechos
Es que debido al alto nivel de excelencia
De nuestros servicios hospitalarios
Los enfermos no mueren oportunamente

Siguen vivos
    aunque en precarias condiciones
Ocasionando múltiples problemas

XIII

REMARKS BY THE MINISTER IN CHARGE

We do not respond
To ill-disposed comments:
Even a nursing child knows
That the tapeworm of extreme poverty
Was caused by previous administrations

We recognize that the unemployment figure
Is somewhat higher than one would like
But we have the responsibility to remind you
That the Government is not an employment agency

There are no lack of beds in the hospitals
It just happens that there are too many sick people...
There's an excessive number of sick in this country
The truth of the matter is
That owing to the high level of excellence
Of our hospital services
The sick are not dying quickly enough

They go on living
                    even if in precarious conditions
Causing numerous difficulties

XIV

EXISTE

Y se llama William Shakespeare
Marlowe
      o Bacon
            o Perico de los Palotes
Hay 40 maneras distintas
De pronunciar esta palabra sagrada

Lo mismo que pasa con la palabra Cervantes
El propio Don Miguel se firmó muchas veces
Con zeta y con belarga

Ya lo dijo mi tía
Shakespeare
          el Cervantes inglés
Cervantes
          el Shakespeare español
El mismo hombre con distintos nombres
Si no existiera habría que inventarlo

Para empezar ambos murieron el mismo día*

*Un 23 de abril como éste
 Si pasamos x alto
 La teoría de los calendarios

XIV

HE EXISTS

And is called William Shakespeare
Marlowe
                    or Bacon
                                        or John Doe
There are 40 different ways
Of pronouncing this sacred word

The same goes for the word Cervantes
Don Miguel himself signed his name many times
With a z and a b

My aunt has already said
Shakespeare
                    the English Cervantes
Cervantes
                    the Spanish Shakespeare
The same man with different names
If he didn't exist we'd have to make him up

To begin with both died the same day*

*A 23rd of April like this one
 If we set aside
 The calendars theory

XV

MACEDONIA

Un joven periodista
Cree reconocer a Borges
En la rambla de Montevideo

Perdone señor
                es Ud. Borges?
Y el venerable anciano respondió:

A veces…

Así era Borges
Una vez alguien tocó el timbre
De su modesto dpto de Buenos Aires

Quién?
                pregunta Borges

Un desconocido de unos 30 años de edad, Sr. Borges
Le contesta su secretario

Y el venerable anciano exclamó:
Cómo!
¿Qué todavía queda gente de 30 años?

Un curioso se le acercó una vez en la calle:
Perdone Sr. Borges
Le podría hacer una pregunta?

Ya la hizo
                respondió Borges
Y apuró el paso

XV

MACEDONIAN FRUIT SALAD

A young journalist
Believes he recognizes Borges
On Montevideo Boulevard

Pardon me sir
                    are you Borges?
And the venerable old man replied:

At times...

Borges was like that
Once someone rang the bell
At his modest apartment in Buenos Aires

Who is it?
                    Borges inquires

His secretary in answering him says
An unknown person of some 30 years of age, Mr. Borges

And the venerable old man exclaimed:
How so!
Are there still people 30 years old?

A curious person once approached him on the street:
Beg your pardon Mr. Borges
Could I ask you a question?

You already have
                    Borges replied
And hurried away

Dejáte de pavadas conmigo Ché:
De uruguacho no tengo
+ que el haber nacido en Buenos Aires
Hijo de padres ricos pero honrados
Macedonio Fernández a la orden
Argentino total hasta la muerte

Don't play your games with me, Ché:
There's nothing about me that's Uruguorphan
Other than having been born in Buenos Aires
The son of rich but honorable parents
Macedonio Fernández at your service
A total Argentine till the day I die

XVI

SÍ

Recuerdo que iba x un camino
De vuelta del trabajo
Cansado como perro
En dirección a mi casa
Cuando de pronto oigo unos martillazos
Y unos quejidos estremecedores

Me desvié algunos pasos
Para imponerme de lo que ocurría
Y en la profundidad de una quebrada
Vi que estaban crucificando a un hombre
De unos 30 años
Esquelético y melenudo

Otros 2 ya habían sido crucificados

Una mujer lloraba arrodillada
Creo que se llamaba Magdalena

Me restregué los ojos y seguí mi camino

—No sintió nada fuera de lo común?
—Nada
Si me detuve algunos minutos
Fue x simple curiosidad

XVI

YES

I remember that I was going down a road
Coming back from work
Dog tired
In the direction of my house
When suddenly I hear some hammer blows
And some frightful moans

I turned aside a few steps
To find out what was happening
And deep in a ravine
I saw they were crucifying a man
Of about 30 years of age
Long-haired and skeletal thin

2 others had already been crucified

A kneeling woman was weeping
I believe her name was Magdalen

I rubbed my eyes and kept going

—You didn't feel anything out of the ordinary?
—Nothing
If I stopped for a few minutes
It was simply out of curiosity

XVII

UNA PREGUNTA AL COMPAÑERO GORBACHOV

Qué razones tuvo
Para cambiar la bandera roja
x la blanca

Yo la hubiera cambiado por la verde

2

Árbol
Lo único que te pido
Es que no me quites el sol

3

¡Incidente
En la Sociedad de Excritores de Chile!
Los poetas se niegan a leer sus poemas
En un momento de descuido
Los autores se dieron a la fuga

4

Escándalos en el cementerio
Tumbas abandonadas
Hurto de flores
Osamentas de cadáveres desconocidos

XVII

A QUESTION FOR COMRADE GORBACHOV

What reasons did you have
For changing the red flag
For a white one

I would have changed it for a green

2

Tree
All that I ask of you
Is that you don't shut out the sun

3

Incident
In the Society of Writurds of Chile!
The poets refuse to read their poems
In a moment of inattention
The authors took to their heels

4

Scandal in the cemetery
Abandoned tombs
Stolen flowers
Bones of unknown cadavers

6

Teatro sin público
Sólo para Dramaturgos
Estrictamente Prohibida la Entrada
Multa   Adultos   1000
               Estudiantes   1500

5

CONTAMINACIÓN
Artefacto dramático

Consiste en quemar un neumático en el escenario
A puertas y ventanas cerradas

9

TEATRO DE OBJETOS
Máquinas al servicio de sí mismas

10

Otro artefacto dramático:

Ordeñar una vaca
Y tirarle la leche x la cabeza

14

Cuando los periodistas
Le preguntaron a la Sexilia Bolocco
x su poeta favorito
La belleza absoluta respondió:

Pongámosle que Shakespeare

6

Theater without patrons
For playwrights only
Entrance strictly forbidden
Fine   Adults   1000
         Students   1500

5

CONTAMINATION
Dramatic artifact

Consists of burning a tire on stage
With doors and windows closed

9

THEATER OF OBJECTS
Machines that serve themselves

10

Another Dramatic Artifact:

Milk a cow
And dump the milk on its head

14

When the journalists
Asked Sexilia Bolocco
To name her favorite poet
The absolute beauty replied:

Let's put down Shakespeare

12

Bueno
Pongámosle que en un comienzo fue el verbo
Y que el verbo estaba en Dios
Y que el verbo era Dios

O nó dicen Uds…

12

Well
Let's put down that in the beginning was the word
And the word was with God
And the word was God

Wouldn't you say...

XVIII

RESUMEN DE LA MATERIA TRATADA HASTA AQUÍ

Cervantes

un principiante que promete mucho

Shakespeare

un jovencito que dará que hablar

XVIII

SUMMARY OF THE SUBJECT MATTER DEALT WITH UP
TO HERE

Cervantes
              a beginner who promises much
Shakespeare
              a young man who will set tongues wagging

XIX

ARTE POÉTICA 1

1% de inspiración
2 de transpiración
& el resto...
                    suerte

XIX

ART OF POETRY 1

1% inspiration
2% perspiration
& the rest...
                luck

XX

ARTE POÉTICA 2

Lo 1º sentarse en el πano
& lo de + sería lo de −

XX

ART OF POETRY 2

The first thing to do is go overboard
& after that nothing would matter*

.

*Translator's note: In the Spanish, the antipoet uses a Chilean expression
that literally says "seat oneself at (or on) the piano," but it means something
like "go beyond the accepted limits." He also plays with "piano" by
employing the mathematical sign for pi in place of the first two letters of
the word.

XXI

TERMINARÉ CON UNA PROPOSICIÓN DESHONESTA

Música maestro:
Propongo que en vez de Teatro de las Naciones
Nos llamemos Teatro del Globo
Dice + & con − palabras

Es un cambio de nombre que se impone
Está a la vista
                no hay x dónde perderse

Recordarase que el Teatro del Globo
Fue construido en 1599 en los suburbios de Londres
Al otro lado del Támesis

Se incendió en 1613
Durante la representación de Henry VIII
Cuyo autor
Estaba x cumplir el medio siglo

Reconstruido en 1614
Estuvo en pie hasta 1644
Año en que lo echaron abajo

Fue demolido...
                "para la construcción de viviendas"
Señala sin inmutarse la Enciclopedia Británica
Negocio redondo por donde se mire

To make a short story long
Yo creí que los ingleses andaban con plumas...

XXI

I WILL END WITH A DISHONEST PROPOSITION

Music maestro:
I propose that instead of Theater of Nations
We call ourselves the Globe Theater
It says more with fewer words

It's a name change that's necessary
It's quite evident
                        there's no way to get confused

Remember that the Globe Theater
Was constructed in 1599 in the London suburbs
On the other side of the Thames

It burned in 1613
During the staging of *Henry VIII*
Whose author
Was about to turn half a century

Reconstructed in 1614
It stood until 1644
The year they tore it down

Demolished it
                "to make way for a housing project"
The *Encyclopedia Britannica* indicates unperturbed
A lucrative deal any way you look at it

To make a short story long:
I believed that the English were savages…

Con razón alguien dijo por ahí*
Nulli mellius piraticam
Exerceunt quam Angli

No hay piratas mejores
Que los ingleses

En Santiago de Chile
A 23 de Abril de 1993

Happy Birthday to him
& 3 ceacheí x el Teatro del Globo!

C,H,I   CHI
L,E   LE

CHI   CHI   CHI
LE   LE   LE

TE − A − TRO − DEL − GLO − BOOOO...

*Scaliger

No wonder someone around here said*
Nulli mellius piraticam
Exerceunt quam Angli

There are no better pirates
Than the English

In Santiago, Chile
On 23 April 1993

Happy birthday to him
& 3 Chile cheers for the Globe Theater!

C,H,I   CHI
L,E   LE

CHI   CHI   CHI
LE   LE   LE

Globe The-a-ter Globe Globe Glooobe…

*Scaliger

ALSO SPRACH ALTAZOR

ALSO SPRACH ALTAZOR

Título del original en inglés
HAY QUE CAGAR A HUIDOBRO

Original title in English:
WE HAVE TO CRAP ON HUIDOBRO

I

ANTES DE COMENZAR

Una pregunta:
Qué sería de Chile sin Huidobro
Qué sería de la chilena poesía sin este duende?
Fácil imaginárselo
Desde luego no habría libertad de expresión
Todos estaríamos escribiendo Sonetos
Odas elementales
                    O gemidos

Alabado sea el Santísimo!

I

WHAT I FEARED WOULD HAPPEN DID

A question:
What would Chile be without Huidobro
What would Chilean poetry be without this duende?
It's easy to imagine
Certainly there would be no freedom of expression
We would all be writing Sonnets
Elemental Odes
        Or moans*

Blessed be the most holy!

*Translator's note: Parra is alluding to Pablo Neruda's *Odas elementales*
 and Pablo de Rokha's first book, *Gemidos.*

II

¿QUÉ DIREMOS DE ÉL

Hoy 10 de enero de 1993
A 100 años de su nacimiento
O de ellos digamos mejor
Porque Huidobros hay en cantidades
Tantos como géneros literarios
                                    y más
Además de los personajes reales
Están los ficticios
En particular ese náufrago
Que nos sonríe desde su paracaídas
Altazor
Un precursor del teniente Bello

La simpatía personificada

II

WHAT SHALL WE SAY OF HIM

Today 10 January 1993
A hundred years since his birth
Or his births we should rather say
Since there are plenty of Huidobros
As many as literary genres
                          and more
In addition to the real types
There are the fictitious
In particular that shipwrecked one
Who smiles at us from his parachute
Altazor
Precursor of Lieutenant Bello*

Likability personified

*Translator's note: Lieutenant Bello was an early Chilean pilot who was lost
  in a fog and whose airplane and body were never found.

III

QUIERO DEJAR EN CLARO

Que sin el maestro no hubiera sido posible el discípulo
Prácticamente todo lo aprendí de Huidobro
Gracias
Incluidas algunas malas costumbres
Ésa es la verdad de las cosas
Las fallas del discípulo no se explican
Sin las genialidades del maestro

III

I WANT TO BE CLEAR

That without the master the disciple would not be possible
I learned practically everything from Huidobro
Thanks
Including some bad habits
That's the truth of the matter
The disciple's faults cannot be explained
Except by the master's eccentricities

IV

ALTAZOR

El esposo de Manuela Portales
El confidente de Teresa de la ✝
El raptor de Ximena Amunátegui
                              Tal cual
El antinovio de Blanca Luz Brun
El otro yo de Raquel Señoret
El galán absoluto según propia declaración
El mejor cocinero del planeta
El campeón de los 100 metros planos
El primer metafísico del Mapocho
El que dejó callado a Pablo de Rokha
Hazaña mayor imposible

El aviador extraviado en la niebla

IV

ALTAZOR

Husband of Manuela Portales
Confidant of Teresa de la ✝
Kidnapper of Ximena Amunátegui

                              To call an ace an ace

Anti-fiancé of Blanca Luz Brun
The other name of Raquel Señoret
The complete lover according to his own assertion
The best cook on earth
Champion of the 100 meters cross country
The first metaphysician of the Mapocho
He who shut up Pablo de Rokha
The greatest impossible feat

The pilot lost in the fog

V

NO TE SIGAS ROMPIENDO LA CABEZA MUCHACHO

Le solía decir su señora madre
Las poesías no las lee nadie

Da lo mismo que sean buenas o malas

V

SON DON'T GO ON BEATING YOUR HEAD AGAINST A WALL

His lady mother used to tell him
Poetry no one reads

It doesn't matter if it's good or bad

VI

COMILLAS

Reconozco que tengo + plata
De la que se puede gastar en Chile

Es por eso que me lo paso viajando

Talento poético nulo
Mi único mérito consiste
En saber reconocer mis errores
En algo sí que soy intransigente
La poesía contemporánea comienza conmigo

Yo soy un aristócrata polaco
Ni una gota de sangre plebeya
Siempre estoy a la altura del azar
He publicado múltiples poesías
En revistas chilenas y extranjeras
A plena satisfacción de los amigos lectores
Y a plena satisfacción de la crítica + exigente
Que la verdad no quede sin ser dicha

VI

IN QUOTES

I realize that I have more money
Than one can spend in Chile

That's why I travel so much

Poetic talent null & void
My only merit consists
In knowing how to recognize my own mistakes
On one score I am uncompromising:
Contemporary poetry begins with me

I am a Polish aristocrat
Not a single drop of plebeian blood
Always rising to take any chance
I have published numerous poems
In Chilean and foreign magazines
To the total satisfaction of reader friends
And the total satisfaction of the most demanding critics
No sense in not telling the truth

VII

¿LOCO? NO SÉ DE QUÉ SE ESCANDALIZAN TANTO

Los locos hacen menos perjuicios que los cuerdos
Unas pocas palabras verdaderas
Y buenas noches los pastores
En cambio los señores sensatos
Nos amargan la vida con sus guerras
Con sus idilios con sus ecuaciones
Alabado sea el Santísimo
Mil veces malo de la cabeza
        ¡qué profesor o padre de la patria!

VII

CRAZY? I DON'T KNOW WHAT
THEY'RE SO SHOCKED ABOUT

The insane do less damage than the sane
A few truthful words
And that's all folks
On the other hand the sensible gentlemen
Embitter our existence with their wars
With their idylls with their equations
Blessed be the most holy
A thousand times off his rocker
            what a professor or founding father!

VIII

NADA DE TRANSACCIONES ACADÉMICAS

Sus opiniones no pecaron nunca de moderadas
Hasta el momento no ha habido ningún poeta
Propiamente tal en el mundo
Incluso llegó a atreverse
A enmendarle la plana al propio Homero
Que no debió haber dicho jamás según él
Las nubes se alejan como un rebaño de ovejas
Sino lisa y sencillamente
Las nubes se alejan balando

Y paré que tenía razón

VIII

NOTHING TO DO WITH ACADEMIC TRANSACTIONS

His opinions never sinned from moderation
Up to now there has been no other poet
Properly such in the world
He even dared
To correct a page of Homer himself
Who according to him never should have said
The clouds move away like a flock of sheep
But rather smoothly and simply
The clouds move off bleating

And it seems that he was right

IX

JUEGOS FLORALES

a la hora de postres

Siempre salía ganador el dueño de casa
Primero Huidobro
Segundo desierto
Tercero Braulio Apenas
Un expoeta joven de la época

Chismología mandragoriana
Amenidades del diario morir

IX

SPRING WRITING FESTIVAL

when dessert is served

Always the master of the house came out the winner
First Huidobro
Second nobody
Third Braulio Apenas*
A young former-poet of the period

Mandragorian gossip-mongering
Pleasantries of the daily dying

*Translator's note: Braulio Arenas (1913-1988) is the Chilean poet to whom
Parra alludes by changing his surname to the word "Apenas," meaning
"Barely." Founder of the Chilean surrealist magazine *Mandrágora*, Arenas
also led a poetry movement of the same name, whose membership
included Teófilo Cid, Enrique Gómez Correa, and Jorge Cáceres.

X

ALTAZOR

Un poema que empieza varias veces
Y no termina nunca de empezar

Una majestuosa catedral inconclusa
La obra gruesa de una catedral
En opinión de Tirios y Troyanos

X

ALTAZOR

A poem that begins several times
And never stops starting

A majestic unfinished cathedral
The skeleton of a cathedral
In the opinion of opposing sides

XI

¿SE CREÍA LA MUERTE EN BICICLETA?

No más que Nietzsche
Bastante menos que Stirner en todo caso
Cuya plataforma de lucha ya no nos llama
Tanto la atención

Recuperación del yo
Completa amoralidad
Y el Club de losEgólatras
El Automóvil Club de losEgólatras
"Der Einzige und sein Eigentum"

Es un error muy grande
Tomar el mundo en serio
La verdadera seriedad es cómica
Trascendencia divina no hay en Huidobro
Trascendencia vacía tampoco
Su inspiración no viene de lo alto
Como muy bien advierte Federico Schopf

XI

DID HE THINK HE WAS THE GREATEST?

No more than Nietzsche
In any case much less than Stirner
Whose plan of attack no longer attracts
Our attention as once it did

Recovery of the I
Complete amorality
And the Club of Self-Worshippers
The Automobile Club of Self-Worshippers
"Der Einzige und sein Eigentum"

It's a very grave error
To take the world seriously
True seriousness is comic
Divine transcendence there's none in Huidobro
Nor empty transcendence either
His inspiration doesn't come from on high
As Federico Schopf so well points out

XII

VALE LA PENA RECORDAR ESO SÍ

Que no se queda nunca donde está
Pronto se pronunció por una poesía escéptica de sí misma
Hasta llegó a dárselas de comunista
Lo fue efectivamente
Ver Elegía a la Muerte de Lenin
Inconmensurable
                    Total
Entre broma y broma
Algunas verdades amargas
Y también tuvo tiempo
Para girar en 180º
En el último tramo de su trayectoria
Convencido que por ahí no iba la cosa

Lucidez y presencia de ánimo

XII

IT'S CERTAINLY WORTH REMEMBERING

That he never stays where he is
Soon he came out in favor of a poetry sceptical of itself
He even played at being a communist
Effectively he was
See his Elegy on the Death of Lenin
Absolutely
               Incomparable
Between jest and joke
A few bitter truths
And also he had time
In the last stretch of his trajectory
To turn around one hundred and eighty degrees
Convinced that things weren't going in that direction

Lucidity and presence of mind

XIII

PALABRAS TEXTUALES

Quien haya estudiado a fondo
El mundo actual
No puede dejar de hacerse comunista

Quien haya estudiado a fondo
El partido comunista
No puede dejar de hacerse anarquista

Believe me
No ser idealista a los 20
Es no tener corazón

Seguir siéndolo a los cuarenta
Es no tener cabeza

XIII

LITERAL WORDS

Whoever may have thoroughly studied
The real world
Cannot help but become a communist

Whoever may have thoroughly studied
The communist party
Cannot help but become an anarchist

Believe me
Not to be an idealist at 20
Is not to have a heart

To go on being one at forty
Is not to have a head

XIV

BORRÓN Y CUENTA NUEVA

Dice
Eli Eli Lama Sabachtani

Debe decir
Con humor y paciencia
Cambiaremos el curso de la historia

XIV

A MISTAKE AND A FRESH START

He says
Eli Eli Lama Sabachtani

He ought to say
With humor and patience
We will change the course of history

XV

EN LA NOMENCLATURA DE EMERSON

Un cobarde que huye para adelante
Ése fue Vicente Huidobro
Cumple con lo que se espera de él:

Es un héroe en toda la extensión de la palabra

XV

IN THE NOMENCLATURE OF EMERSON

A coward who flees ahead
That was Vicente Huidobro
Doing his duty as to whatever's expected of him:

He's a hero in every sense of the word

XVI

SE LE TILDÓ

Qué no se le tildó
                    de noctámbulo
De payaso
                    de pije
                              de rastacuero
Todos los epítetos imaginables
Incluido el + ofensivo de todos
Hay que borrarlo como sea del mapa
Léase
Hay que cagar a Huidobro
No sé
Estamos en Chile
Faltan palabras en el Diccionario

XVI

ACCUSED HIM OF

What didn't they accuse him of
                                        night owl
Clown
                        shabby-genteel
                                                Francophile
All the epithets imaginable
Including the most offensive of all
One way or another he has to be erased from the map
That is
One has to crap on Huidobro
I don't know
We're in Chile
Not enough words for it in the dictionary

XVII

¿TANGO DE VIUDO?

Para tangos me quedo con Gardel

XVII

THE WIDOWER'S TANGO?

As to tangos I'll stick with Gardel*

*Translator's note: "The Widower's Tango" is the English version of Pablo Neruda's poem, "Tango del viudo," which forms part of his *Residencia en la tierra* (1933). Faride Zerán's book, *La Guerrilla literaria: Huidobro, de Rokha, Neruda,* traces the literary warfare waged among this trio of Chilean poets. Parra terms their "guerrilla" activity "poetomaquia" ("poetomachy" or "poetfighting"), a play on "tauromaquia," the Spanish word for bullfighting. Alluding to Neruda's poem, "The Widower's Tango," Huidobro had said that he preferred the tangos of the great Argentine singer-composer Carlos Gardel, implying his disdain for Neruda's brand of poetry. This long note applies not only to this one-line section but to section XXIII, as well as to other of Parra's allusions to the infighting that took place during the 1930s among three of Chile's "leading contenders."

XVIII

ALGUIEN ANDA DICIENDO X AHÍ

Que cuando Vicentito se pone insolente
Cosa que ocurre bien a menudo
Poco se gana con bajar la voz
Arriba los corazones
Ha llegado la hora del recto al mentón

XVIII

SOMEBODY GOES AROUND SAYING

That when little Vicente turns insolent
Something that happens frequently
It doesn't help much to lower one's voice
Take heart
It's time for an uppercut to the jaw

XIX

OJOS EN TINTA

Dientes de menos
Y vamos viendo qué es la poesía
Cada *maffia* tenía sus matones
Diego Muñoz
                   Tomás
                             Orlando Oyarzún
Y Cía ilimitada

XIX

BLACK EYES

Teeth missing
And we go on seeing what poetry is
Every mafia had its heavies
Diego Muñoz
              Tomás
                      Orlando Oyarzún
And Co. Unlimited

XX

NERUDIANA

Huidobro está a la cabeza
De una maniobra internacional anti Neruda
Pero yo voy a dejar caer todo mi poder
Que es muy grande
En la cabeza del señor Huidobro!

Dicho y hecho

XX

NERUDIANA

Huidobro is at the head
Of an international anti-Neruda operation
But I am going to let all my power
Which is very great
Fall on Mr. Huidobro's head!

No sooner said than done

XXI

LÁSTIMA QUE NERUDA

Haya terminado pisando el palito
No tenía perno para esa tuerca
Era poeta lírico
                  no dramático
No sabía pelear a puño limpio
No manejaba bien la margarita

Se veía mejor en la penumbra

XXI

TOO BAD THAT NERUDA

Should have ended up falling in the trap
He didn't have the bolt that fit the nut
He was a lyric poet
                    not a dramatic
He didn't know how to fight bare-fisted
He couldn't hold his liquor

He looked better in twilight shadows

XXII

DEMASIADAS ESTRELLAS

Al Creador se le pasó la mano
Con la mitad hubiera habido de sobra

XXII

TOO MANY STARS

The Creator overdid it
Half as many would have been more than enough

XXIII

CLARO QUE ÉL SABÍA DEFENDERSE

Pobre del quiltro o del perro de raza
Que le saliera a ladrar al camino
Ver La Poetomaquia de Faride Zerán

Una vez le enrostraron
Que su abuelo el Marqués de Casa Real
Se había hecho rico durante la Colonia
Comerciando en esclavos

Prefiero descender de mi abuelo
Que trajo esclavos replicó
A descender como Uds.
De los esclavos que trajo mi abuelo

XXIII

HE SURE KNEW HOW TO DEFEND HIMSELF

A poor little mutt or a registered breed
Who'd run out to bark in the street
Consult the Poetfighting of Faride Zerán

Once they threw in his face
That his grandfather the Marquis de Casa Real
Had made himself rich during Colonial days
Trading in slaves

I prefer to descend from my grandfather
Who brought over slaves he said
Than to descend as you
From the slaves brought over by grandpa

XXIV

YO NO VEO COMO UN ARISTÓCRATA

Pueda escribir poesía
Declaró públicamente Alguien alguna vez

A lo que el gran Huidobro retrucó:
Yo no veo que para escribir poesía
Se tenga que ser hijo de ferroviario

XXIV

I DON'T SEE HOW AN ARISTOCRAT

Can be capable of writing poetry
One time Someone declared in public

To which the great Huidobro shot back:
I don't see why in order to write poetry
One has to be the son of a railway man

XXV

LAS HISTORIETAS FALSAS O VERDADERAS

Crecen en progresión geométrica
En casi todas sale victorioso

Se me tilda de ególatra
Habría dicho una vez
Porque me defiendo como gato de espaldas

En mi sagrado derecho que estoy

Que me choreen el reloj
                    en buena hora
La billetera?
                no me preocupa!
Sé que les hace falta
Pero que me respeten la camisa
No?

XXV

TALES TRUE OR FALSE

Grow in geometric progression
In almost every one he comes out victorious

They accuse me of self-worship
He once might have said
Since I defend myself like a cat on its back

I'm within my sacred rights

Let them steal my watch
                              that's fine
My billfold?
                    doesn't matter to me!
I know they need it
But let them spare my shirt
No?

XXVI

CIERTA VEZ TUVO LA OCURRENCIA

De disfrazarse de mendigo
Y se puso a pedir limosna
En la puerta de la Catedral

Pronto se le acercó
El sacerdote mayor en persona
Agitando en el aire una moneda de plata
Que Huidobro rechaza dignamente
Con una frase lapidaria que se hará célebre:

RETÍRATE EGÓLATRA!

XXVI

ONE TIME IT OCCURRED TO HIM

To dress up like a mendicant
And he set about begging for alms
In front of the cathedral door

He was soon approached
By the principal priest
Shaking in the air a silver coin
Which Huidobro rejects with dignity
Uttering a precise elegant phrase later celebrated:

HENCE EGOTIST!

XXVII

PSEUDÓNIMO

No tengo nada que ocultar exclamó
Que se cambien de nombre los sospechosos
Yo desciendo directamente del Cid

XXVII

PSEUDONYM

I don't have anything to hide he exclaimed
Let the suspects change their names
I descend directly from The Cid*

*Translator's note: The names of a number of Chilean poets were
pseudonyms, including Gabriela Mistral, Pablo Neruda, and Pablo de
Rokha. Huidobro claimed to be related to the subject of the great medieval
Spanish epic, *Poema del Cid*, and he wrote his version of the epic hero's
life in his novel entitled *Mío Cid Campeador* (1926). See section XXVIII.

XXVIII

CAMPEADOR & SABIO DON VICENTE

Como buen tataranieto de don Alfonso
En efecto
Fuera de las cabezas que cortó
Resolvió dos problemas insolubles:
El de la curvatura del círculo
Ver Horizon Carré
Y el Problema del Movimiento Perpetuo:

Nunca se estableció en ninguna parte

3 efectivamente
Ya que como se dijo + arriba
Goza de juventud inalterable

Todo bajo control

El Problema del Vellocino de Oro
Ya lo había resuelto su abuelito
Dueño de medio Chile
De la Plaza de Armas por lo muy menos

XXVIII

CAMPEADOR & SAPIENT DON VICENTE

As a good great-great-grandson of Alfonso
As it were
Aside from the heads cut off
He solved two insoluble problems:
The one of Squaring the Circle
See his Horizon Carré*
And the Problem of Perpetual Motion:

He never settled down anywhere

3 effectively
Since as was stated above
He enjoys eternal youth

Everything under control

The Problem of the Golden Fleece
His grandfather had already solved
Owner of half of Chile
Of the Plaza of Arms at the very least

*Translator's note: *Horizon Carré* is a book of Huidobro's poems in French;
the title means square horizon (or circle).

XXIX

ASÍ ERA HUIDOBRO

No me pidan que escriba con los pies
Replicó
Cuando se le tildó de cerebral

El rigor verdadero reside en la cabeza

Que Neruda se haga cargo de las empleadas domésticas

Esta es una poesía para príncipes

XXIX

HUIDOBRO WAS LIKE THAT

Don't ask me to write with my feet
He replied
When they accused him of being too intellectual

True rigor resides in the head

Let Neruda be in charge of housemaids

This is a poetry for princes

XXX

NI DADAÍSTA NI SURREALISTA

Ni futurista
                ni mundonovista
Ni masoquista
                ni social realista
Creacionista mujer x Dios
El poeta es un pequeño Dios
Un pequeño demonio
                c'est la même chose

Conste
Que yo no tengo nada contra ti
Eres una viejita encantadora
Pero déjame hacer mis propios ríos
Mis propios árboles
                mis propios volcanes
Tal como tú pariste los tuyos
Tengo tanto derecho como tú
Soy tu hijo
                tu nieto
                        lo reconozco
Pero ya llegué a mi mayoría de edad
Chao
        lo siento mucho
                        te quiero mucho
Madrenaturaleza
                        Abuelitanaturaleza
No te enojes conmigo

XXX

NEITHER DADAIST NOR SURREALIST

Nor futurist
    nor newworldist
Nor masochist
    nor social realist
By God woman a Creationist
The poet is a little God*
A little devil
    it's the same thing

Be assured
That I have nothing against you
You're an enchanting little old lady
But let me make my own rivers
My own trees
    my own volcanoes
Just as you gave birth to yours
I have as much right as you
I am your son
    your grandson
        I acknowledge it
But I have come of age
Bye-Bye
    I'm sorry
        I love you dearly
Mothernature
    Grandmothernature
Don't be angry with me

*Translator's note: This famous line comes from Huidobro's poem, "Ars poética."

XXXI

QUIÉN ES PRIMERO EL HUEVO O LA GALLINA

Problema metafísico de proporciones
Huidobro o Reverdy
Carlos Díaz o Pablo de Rokha
Neruda o Rabindranath Tagore

Ofrezco la palabra

XXXI

WHICH COMES FIRST THE EGG OR THE CHICKEN

Metaphysical problem of vast proportions
Huidobro or Reverdy
Carlos Díaz or Pablo de Rokha
Neruda or Rabindranath Tagore

I yield the floor

XXXII

VINCENT HUIDOBRO

Par lui même
poète français
Né au Chili

XXXII

VINCENT HUIDOBRO

All the same to him
French poet
Born in Chile

XXXIII

DEMIURGO

Genio maléfico que creó el mundo
Contra la voluntad de Dios
Según el canon valentinista
Con el objetivo siniestro
De parcelar el alma universal

(Enciclopédico Hispanoamericano)

Me pregunto si Huidobro…
Completen uds. mismos la frase

Yo diría que no
De todos modos se hace acreedor
A un buen tironcito de orejas
De parte de N.S.M.I.C.
Por esas ínfulas de Pequeño Dios o Demiurgo

Oremus

XXXIII

DEMIURGE

Maleficent genius who created the world
Against the will of God
According to Valentinian law
With the sinister intent
Of parceling out the universal soul

(Hispanic American Encyclopedia)

I ask myself if Huidobro...
You complete the phrase

I would say no
In any case he does deserve
A good ear-pulling
On the part of our Holy Mother Church
Just for those conceits of Little God or Demiurge

Let us pray

XXXIV

NON SERVIAM

Aló?
Nos despedimos del pasado remoto
Fin a la mimesis
A la catarsis
A la capacidad negativa
A espejo que se pasea por el paisaje

Good bye to ALL THAT

Ahora viene el Creacionismo
O poesía propiamente tal

Huifa!

XXXIV

NON SERVIAM

Hello?
We bid farewell to the remote past
The end of mimesis
Of catharsis
Of negative capability
Of the looking glass that promenades through the landscape

Good bye to ALL THAT

Now comes Creationism
Or poetry properly such

Whoopee!

XXXV

¿PALABRAS EN LIBERTAD?

¿Álgebra de metáforas?
Un galimatías sin pies ni cabeza
Jerigonza
+ fácil de escribir que de leer
En opinión de Jenaro Prieto

XXXV

WORDS AT LIBERTY?

Algebra of metaphors?
A headless tailless rigmarole
Gibberish
Easier to write than read
In the opinion of Jenaro Prieto

XXXVI

RENUNCIAR A LA MÉTRICA Y A LA RIMA

Reemplazar la cámara fotográfica x el caleidoscopio
No mirar para atrás
Hacer subir una vaca x el arco iris
El volantín como medio de locomoción
Orinar en un tarro parafinero
Negocio redondo por donde se mire

Publicar los poemas
En rollos de papel higiénico
Por supuesto sras & sres
Ediciones biodegradables
Sensacional
                genial
                        elefantástico!
Negocio redondo por donde se mire

Pero no nos vengan con que eso es poesía

XXXVI

TO RENOUNCE METER AND RHYME

To replace the photographic camera with the kaleidoscope
Not to look back
To make a cow climb on the rainbow
The kite as a means of locomotion
To urinate in a paraffin pot
Smashing success from any angle

To publish poems
On rolls of toilet paper
Certainly ladies & gentlemen
In biodegradable editions
Sensational
                    ingenious
                                        elephantastic!
Smashing success from any angle

But don't try to tell us that's poetry

XXXVII

QUÉ ES POESÍA

La fundación del ser x la palabra
Poesía eres tú
Todo lo que se mueve es poesía
Lo que no cambia de lugar es prosa

Pero qué es poesía
Todo lo que nos une es poesía
Sólo la prosa puede separarnos

Sí pero qué es poesía
Vida en palabras
Un enigma que se niega a ser descifrado x los profesores
Un poco de verdad y una aspirina
Antipoesía eres tú

XXXVII

WHAT IS POETRY?

Existence based on the word
Poetry are you
Everything that moves is poetry
What doesn't change places is prose

But what is poetry
Everything that unites us is poetry
Only prose can keep us apart

Yes but what is poetry
Life in words
An enigma that refuses to be deciphered by professors
A bit of truth and an aspirin
Antipoetry are you

XXXVIII

PARA COMPLICAR OTRO POCO LAS COSAS

Conviene tener presente
Que también hay un Huidobro convencional
Admirador sincero
De un Modernismo de 2º orden
Un promotor apasionado de...
Pedro Antonio González!
El poeta de Chile según él

Lo que oyen señoras y señores!

¿Y Magallanes y Pezoa Véliz?
Nos preguntamos nosotros con rabia
¡Como si nunca hubieran existido!

XXXVIII

TO COMPLICATE THINGS A BIT MORE

It's fitting to bear in mind
That there's also a conventional Huidobro
Sincere admirer
Of a second-rate Modernism
A passionate promoter of…
Pedro Antonio González!
The poet of Chile according to him

You heard right ladies & gentlemen!

What about Magallanes and Pezoa Véliz?
We angrily ask ourselves
As if they never existed!

XXXIX

CONCHAS Y CARACOLAS DEL POETA

Completísima la colección
Acota Maese de Rokk

Sólo le falta la de la mamá

XXXIX

THE POET'S CONCHES AND SHELLS

The most complete collection
Master de Rokk admits

Only his mother's is missing*

*Translator's note: "Concha" in Spanish is both conch shell and pudenda.

XL

W.C. POEM

Poeta soy y me llamo Pablo
Mi razón está en mi locura
Nieto de Dios Hijo del Diablo
Y con ganas de hacerme cura

+ Respeto   – Basura
Pienso & escribo como hablo
Me 100to en la literatura

XL

W.C. POEM

Poet I am and Pablo's my name
My reason lies in my insanity
Grandson of God Son of Satan
Eager to become a parish priest

More respect   less Rubbish
I think & write as I speak
I shit on the literary itch*

*Translator's note: Typical of the antipoet's paradoxical rejection of
literature even as he makes it, this line in Spanish combines the sound of
the number one-hundred (*cien* when spelled out) with the last syllable of
the word *siento*. Both *cien* and *sien* share the same sound, so that with *to*
added to one-hundred, Parra creates the word *siento*, which means "I sit"
or "I seat." *Siento* plus *me* (me or myself) and *en* (on) can signify
figuratively "I shit" or "I crap" on something – here, the making of
literature, and specifically the poetry of Pablo de Rokha. All of this relates
to the poem title: W.C. (Water Closet or toilet).

XLI

NO CONDENAR A PRIORI LA VIOLENCIA

Determine primero
De qué tipo de violencia se trata
Justa o injusta
Porque cuando la violencia es justa
Qué quiere que le diga pues compadre:

Es simplemente justa la violencia

XLI

NOT TO CONDEMN VIOLENCE AHEAD OF TIME

Determine first
What kind of violence is involved
Just or unjust
Because when the violence is just
What do you want me to say my friend:

The violence is simply just

XLII

1935

Pablo de Rokha
Le declara la Guerra a Muerte
Problemas fronterizos

Una guerra perdida de antemano
Como toda guerra que se respete

Pobre mulato Taguá no sabía la chicha
                         con que se estaba curando

XLII

1935

Pablo de Rokha
Declares a Fight to the Death
Border conflicts

A war lost beforehand
Like every war one can respect

Poor mulatto Taguá didn't know who
                                   he was messing with

XLIII

LOS 3

Eran admiradores de Rimbaud
Incondicionales si no me equivoco
Pero díganme Uds
Cuál de los 3 enloqueció a Verlaine
Cuál de los 3 se hizo amputar una pierna

Ninguno que yo sepa
Qué discípulos más independientes!

Y la pregunta del millón de dólares

Cuál de los 3 se hizo el harakiri
Cuál de los 3 dejó de escribir a los 20

Yo comienzo a leer a los 80

XLIII

THE 3

Were devotees of Rimbaud
Unconditionally so if I'm not mistaken
But you tell me
Which of the 3 drove Verlaine insane
Which of the 3 had his leg amputated

Not one as far as I know
What disciples more unfaithful!

And the million dollar question

Which of the 3 committed hara-kiri
Which of the 3 quit writing at twenty

At eighty I'm beginning to read

XLIV

LAZ COZAZ X ZU NOMBRE

Cuando salió la Antología
Pablo de Rokha puso el grito en el cielo
Le pareció que se le sub estimaba

Acusó de Eminencia Gris a Huidobro

Pobre pollo
Se le fueron las plumas a la cabeza
Bravuconadas subidas de tono
Golpes bajos a diestra y siniestra
Hasta que Huidobro perdió la paciencia

Y fue el comienzo de La Poetomaquia

Muy ingenioso
                muy escandaloso
Pero Huidobro lo dejó callado

Sensacional
                genial
                        elefantástico

Pero Huidobro
Como que se lo anduvo madrugando
Daba vergüenza ajena
Ver al campeón de todos los pesos
Echando sangre por boca y narices

XLIV

THINGZ BY ZEIR NAMEZ

When the Anthology came out
Pablo de Rokha raised such a ruckus
To his mind it rated him far too low

He accused Huidobro of underhanded machinations

Poor ducky
His pen feathers went to his head
Intense swaggering tones
Low blows right and left
Till Huidobro lost his patience

And so began the Poetfighting

Very ingenious
                    very scandalous
But Huidobro shut him up

Sensational
              ingenious
                          elephantastic!

But Huidobro
Was one step ahead
And it left one feeling embarrassed
To see the boxing champ of every weight
Bleeding through his mouth and nose

XLV

EN PRIVADO & EN PÚBLICO

Le sacaron la madre varias veces
No le quedaba otra que partir
O matar
      O pegarse un tiro

XLV

IN PRIVATE & IN PUBLIC

Several times they insulted his mother
There was nothing he could do but leave
Or kill someone
        Or shoot himself

XLVI

PALABRAS TEXTUALES

Este país no tiene remedio
Saben que son imbéciles y sonríen
Satisfechos
                    los pobres infelices
Tropa de sifilíticos alcohólicos
Por un hombre de buenos sentimientos
Un millón de huasos macucos

Ésa es la proporción
Especialistas
En herir al prójimo x la espalda
Nunca atacan de frente los cobardes
La puñalada siempre por la espalda
Pero a mí no me van a destruir
Estos mediocres
                    estos alacranes

Estos reptiles de ojos vidriosos

Tengo alas señoras & señores
A París
          a Madrid
                    adonde sea
Lo + lejos posible
                    Para siempre!
No me quedo ni un día + aquí

Música maestro!...

XLVI

LITERAL WORDS

This country is beyond redemption
They know they're imbeciles and yet they smile
Self-satisfied
       the pitiful wretches
A troop of syphilitic alcoholics
For every man with a sense of duty
A million cunning rednecks

That's the ratio
Specialists
In stabbing their fellows in the back
The cowards never attack face to face
Always the knife when one's not looking
But they're never going to cut me down
These incompetents
          these scorpions

These glassy-eyed reptiles

I have wings ladies & gents
To Paris
      to Madrid
            to wherever it may be
As far away as possible
          Forever!
I won't stay here one more day

Music maestro!...

XLVII

UNA SOLA PREGUNTA

Se acostó o no se acostó
Con la Teresa de la ✝

Solamente una vez

                    Se ama en la vida
Con la dulce y total renunciación
Una vez nada + en la vida brilló la esperanza
La esperanza que alumbra el camino de mi soledad

XLVII

JUST ONE QUESTION

Did he sleep or didn't he sleep
With Teresa de la ♱

Only once

       Does one ever love in life
With sweet and complete surrender
Once & never more in life did hope shine forth
The hope that lights my lonely road*

*Translator's note: Beginning with "Only once" the antipoet is quoting a
bolero by Mexican composer Agustín Lara.

XLVIII

ESTÁ A LA VISTA

Que se sobregiraban los muchachos
Ímpetus juveniles
                              o algo por el estilo

Se creían la muerte en bicicleta
¡Qué lástima

Happy Birthday anyway

XLVIII

IT IS EVIDENT

That the boys had overdrawn their accounts
Impetuous youths
                    or something of the sort

Thought they were hot stuff
Too bad

Happy Birthday anyway

XLIX

QUISIERA DEDICAR ESTA NOTA

Si ustedes me lo permiten
A la memoria de Ángel Cruchaga
Por la primera estrofa de ese poema
Que nos sabemos todos de memoria:

En mi silencio azul lleno de barcos
Sólo tu rostro vive
En el mar de la tarde el día duerme
Eres más bella cuando estoy más triste

Parece el joven Neruda no?
Pero es el viejo Ángel Cruchaga Santa María

Se da la casualidad
De que también está de centenario
Como Teresa de la ✝
              como Pedro Siena
Como Álvaro Yánez
El inconmensurable Juan Emar
¡Faltan coronas para tantos muertos!

XLIX

I WOULD LIKE TO DEDICATE THIS NOTE

If you will permit me
To the memory of Ángel Cruchaga
For the first stanza of that poem
Which we've all gotten by heart:

In my blue silence full of ships
Your face alone is living
In the sea of evening the day sleeps on
When I am sad you are even more lovely

Sounds like the young Neruda doesn't it?
But it's old Ángel Cruchaga Santa María

It just so happens
That it's the centennial
Of Teresa de la ✞
                    of Pedro Sienna
Of Álvaro Yáñez
The incomparable Juan Emar
Not enough wreaths for so many dead!

L

NO SON POCOS LOS CRÍTICOS

Que lo situan x encima de todos
Para muchos
El autor de Altazor
Es el poeta máximo del nuevo mundo

Las opiniones están divididas
Dirán Uds
Ese lugar le corresponde a Ezra Pound
A Whitman
                    a Vallejo
                                a Drummond de Andrade
Para no mencionar a los nerudianos
Que fueron siempre los más poderosos
El oro de Moscú pues
Y la Mistral?
                    Insondable misterio…

El modernismo sigue en el poder
Señala Habermas
A pesar de que ya se desintegró
Como manera de pensar el mundo

L

THERE'S NO SCARCITY OF CRITICS

Who place him above all others
For many
The author of Altazor
Is the new world's greatest poet

The opinions are divided
Some of you will say
That position belongs to Ezra Pound
To Whitman
    to Vallejo
        to Drummond de Andrade
Not to mention the Nerudians
Who were always the most powerful
The Moscow gold, don't you know
And Mistral?
      Unfathomable mystery...

Modernism is still in vogue
Habermas has indicated
Despite the fact that as a way of thinking about the world
It disintegrated

LI

1993

A pocos metros del tercer milenio
Temor e incertidumbre
Una de las pocas cosas
Que podemos decir a ciencia cierta
Es que los años pasan a favor de Huidobro
Se le celebran en todas sus humoradas
Y él nos perdona todas nuestras dudas

LI

1993

Just meters away from the Third Millenium
Dread and uncertainty
One of the few things
We can say for sure
Is that the years go on in Huidobro's favor
With all his witty sayings celebrated
And he forgiving us for all our doubts

LII

HAY UNA FRASE DE VICENTE HUIDOBRO

Que siempre me llamará la atención
No creo que haya otra más enigmática
Más sobrecogedora
                    más terrible
En todo el reino de las Bellas Letras:

Una mujer descuartizada
Viene cayendo desde hace 140 años

A mí me deja mudo

LII

THERE'S A VICENTE HUIDOBRO PHRASE

That will always grab my attention
I don't believe there is any other so enigmatic
More awe-inspiring
                              more frightening
In all the realm of Belle Lettres:

A quartered woman
Has been falling for 140 years

It leaves me speechless

LIII

OTRA

Las amapolas que comemos
Hablan x nosotros

LIII

ANOTHER

The red poppies we eat
Through us do speak

LIV

FRASES PARA EL BRONCE

Vengan o no vengan al caso
Se multiplican hasta el infinito

La idea parece consistir
En sorprender
A esa mujer llamada Re- llamada Re- Realidad
Esa puta llamada realidad
En sus momentos de descuido
Que son los momentos
En que ella se deja penetrar
Hasta verte Cristo mío
Comillas:
Esa rueda que sigue girando después de la catástrofe
El barco que se hunde sin apagar las luces
El eco de mi voz hace tronar el caos
Y al fondo de las olas
Un pez escucha el paso de los hombres

LIV

PHRASES TO ENGRAVE IN BRONZE

Whether they are relevant or not
They multiply in number to infinity

The idea seems to consist
In surprising
That woman called Re- called Re- Reality
That whore called reality
In her unguarded moments
Which are the moments
When she allows penetration
Up to the hilt
Quotation marks:
That wheel that continues turning after the catastrophe
The ship that's sunk without its lights going out
The echo of my voice makes chaos thunder
And at the bottom of the waves
A fish listens to the passing of men*

*Translator's note: Parra is quoting lines from Cantos I and II of Huidobro's
Altazor or The Parachute Voyage.

LV

LOS LECTORES ESCÉPTICOS

Que se resisten
A ver en él un profeta en su tierra
Podrían darse el lujo de volver a leer
Altazor
      Canto I
            Versículos 469-489

La dimensión ecológica de Huidobro
No debiera seguir pasándose por alto así como así

LV

THE SCEPTICAL READERS

Who resist
Seeing in him a prophet in his own land
Could afford to read again
Altazor
      Canto I
             Verses 469-489

The ecological dimension of Huidobro
Should no longer be so easily ignored

LVI

TOTAL CERO

Todo se redujo a nada
Y de la nada va quedando poco

Oremus

El error consistió
En creer que la tierra era nuestra
Cuando la realidad de las cosas
Es que nosotros somos
                         de
                              la
                                   tierra

LVI

TOTAL ZERO

Everything was reduced to nothing
And of the nothing little remains

Let us pray

The error consisted
In believing the earth was ours
When the truth of the matter is
That we belong
                    to
                        the
                            earth

LVII

DESAUTORIZADOS POR ANACRÓNICOS

Los que vieron en él
Un petimetre de la Place Vendôme

Puestos en su lugar
Quienes lo estigmatizaron de Yanacona
De narciso
            de pije
                        de vendepatria
Hay que tomarlo en serio
                             no queda otra
Por escasa que sea la confianza que inspira
Según el solitario crítico dominical*

Hoy por hoy no nos merece ninguna duda
Hasta los bolcheviques se matriculan con él

*Alone (Hernán Díaz Arrieta)

LVII

DISCREDITED AS ANACRONISTS

Those who saw in him
A dandy from the Place Vendôme

Put in their places
Those who stigmatized him as an Indian sharecropper
A narcissus
        a shabby-genteel
                      an unpatriotic fop
We have to take him seriously
               there's no alternative
Regardless of how little trust he inspires
According to the lone Sunday critic*

For the present time he shouldn't be doubted at all
Behind him even the Bolsheviks fall in line

*Alone (Hernán Díaz Arrieta)

283

LVIII

PERSONAJE DIFÍCIL DE ENCASILLAR ES HUIDOBRO

Recuerda a ese caballo
Que se agranda a medida que se aleja

No respeta la ley de la perspectiva

Cómo se explica Sr Alcalde
Que no se le haya erigido una estatua!
Aunque él se reía de las estatuas
Una calle
      un museo
            cualquier cosa…
Hasta cuándo vamos a seguir ninguneándolo!
Por qué no se reeditan sus Obras Completas!
Ediciones populares no hay!

Cómo se explica
Sr Presidente de la Sociedad de Escritores de Chile
Que no le den el Premio Nacional
So pretexto de que está muerto!

Ojalá los amigos sepultureros
Estuvieran tan vivos como él

Qué vergüenza + grande!
Ni Nacional

LVIII

HUIDOBRO'S A DIFFICULT FIGURE TO CLASSIFY

Remember that horse
That grows larger the farther it moves away*

He doesn't respect the law of linear perspective

How explain Mr. Mayor
That no statue has been erected to him!
Even though he laughed at statues
A street
     a museum
          anything whatever...
How much longer will we go on making him a nobody!
Why not republish his Complete Works!
There's not even a trade edition!

How explain
Mr. President of the Society of Chilean Writers
That they may not give him the National Prize
Under the pretext of his being dead!

Would that his grave-digging friends
Were as alive as he!

What a crying shame
Not the National

*Translator's note: The reference here is to Huidobro's line in *Altazor* that
reads: "Un caballo que se va agrandando a medida que se aleja." See
The Selected Poetry of Vicente Huidobro, ed. David M. Guss (New York:
New Directions, 1981), p. 108.

Ni Nobel
Ni siquiera Municipal!

Todavía hay gente que cree en los premios!

Not the Nobel
Not even the Municipal!

There are still people who believe in awards!

LIX

OTRA IMAGEN DE LO QUE REPRESENTA HUIDOBRO

La da ese árbol que tenía miedo
De distanciarse mucho de la tierra
Pánico
De separarse mucho de la tierra

Le dolían las hojas y las raíces

Odiaba a los pájaros
Que se ponían a cantar en sus ramas

LIX

ANOTHER IMAGE OF WHAT HUIDOBRO REPRESENTS

The one of that tree that was afraid
To go very far from the earth
Panicky
Of being much separated from earth

Its leaves and roots ached

It hated the birds
That began singing in its limbs

LX

EN RESUMEN

En síntesis
          en muchas palabras

Poeta
Antipoeta
& mago
      o insecto Perfecto

Lo que oyen señoras y señores
& lo de + sería lo de −
Una sola pregunta
Al autor de Adiós Poeta
Cuándo piensa escribir
Buenos Días Antipoeta

Ya estaría bueno
La paciencia también tiene su límite

LX

TO SUM UP

To synthesize
          in many words

Poet
Antipoet
& magician
      or Perfect Insect

You heard it ladies and gentlemen
& all the rest is meaningless
Just one question
Of the author of Goodbye Poet
When do you plan to write
Good Morning Antipoet

It's about time
Patience too has its limits

LXI

ANTIPOETA VICENTE HUIDOBRO?

Chanfle!
Yo tenía entendido
Que el inventor de la antipoesía
Había sido otro

Comunista además?
Me desayuno x segunda vez

Y pobre como la rata…
Nó!
Me desayuno por tercera y última vez

Está a la vista que El Mercurio miente
No le crean a Parra ni a Valente

LXI

VICENTE HUIDOBRO AN ANTIPOET?

You're kidding!
I had understood
That the inventor of antipoetry
Was someone else

A communist to boot?
That's the first I heard of it

And poor as a rat...
No!
For the third and last time that's news to me

It's clear that El Mercurio lies
Don't believe either Parra or Valente*

*Translator's note: Ignacio Valente is a priest-critic for the major Chilean newspaper, *El Mercurio*, in whose pages Valente has long analyzed and praised Parra's antipoetry.

LXII

EL QUE MURIÓ MÁS JOVEN FUE HUIDOBRO

A los 55
Lihn a los 58
La Mistral a los 68
Neruda a los 69

Moraleja:
Los inmortales no llegan a los 70

Me pregunto qué hubiera pasado con él
De no mediar el accidente fatal

Ofrezco la palabra
Pólvora le quedaba para rato
El reloj de Caronte se adelanta + de la cuenta

LXII

THE YOUNGEST TO DIE WAS HUIDOBRO

At 55
Lihn at 58
Mistral at 68
Neruda at 69

Moral:
Immortals don't make it to 70

I ask myself what would have come of him
Had not the fatal accident occurred

I yield the floor
He still had plenty of fire in the belly
Caronte's watch runs faster than it should

LXIII

DESDE EL BALCÓN DE MI CASA

Veo la tumba de Vicente Huidobro
Resplandecer al otro lado de la bahía

De la mañana a la noche percibo
Las señales eléctricas del poeta

Amanece y se pone con el sol

LXIII

FROM THE BALCONY OF MY HOUSE

I can see Vicente Huidobro's tomb
Shining on the other side of the bay

From morning to night I perceive
The poet's electric signals

He rises and sets with the sun

LXIV

DOS VECES EN LA HIA DE CHILE*

Un poeta mayor ha sido candidato
A la Presidencia de la República

Huidobro en 1925
Con el apoyo de la Federación de Estudiantes

Se siente Vicente
Huidobro Presidente

& el paPablo en 1970
Candidato de la hoz y el martillo

Con ayuda o sin ayuda
Triunfaremos con Neruda

De suceder lo que no sucedió
Nos hubiéramos economizado la Dictadura tal vez
Y la Matanza del Seguro Obrero

O no dicen Uds...?

*La tercera será la vencida

LXIV

TWICE IN THE HIST OF CHILE*

A major poet has been a candidate
For Presidency of the Republic

Huidobro in 1925
With the backing of the Student Federation

Vicente feels
He's Presidential

& the paPablo in 1970
Candidate of the hammer & sickle

With help or without help
With Neruda we'll prevail

To have happened what didn't happen
We would have been spared perhaps the Dictatorship
And the Massacre at the Workers Pension Hall

Or don't you think...?

*The third time will be the charm

LXV

NADA DEL OTRO MUNDO

Macedonio también fue candidato
A la Presidencia de la República
Claro que en broma
Huidobro lo fue en serio lamentablemente
Tan en serio o + que el autor
De pResidencia en la Tierra
No?

Otro punto a favor de Macedonio
Su poesía no la entiende nadie

LXV

NOTHING SPECIAL

Macedonio was also a candidate
For the Republic's President
But surely just as a joke
Sadly Huidobro was dead serious
As serious or more so than the author
Of pResidency on Earth
No?

Another point in favor of Macedonio
Nobody understands his poetry

LXVI

¿ES UD URUGUAYO DON JORGE?

Dejáte de pavadas conmigo ché:
De uruguayo no tengo
+ que el haber nacido en Buenos Aires
Hijo de padres ricos ... pero honrados

Argentino total hasta la muerte

LXVI

SIR JORGE ARE YOU URUGUAYAN?

Enough with the inane questions ché:
I have no more Uruguayan in me
Than having been born in Buenos Aires:
Son of rich ... but honorable parents

Pure Argentinian till the day I die

LXVII

UNA VEZ EN LA RAMBLA DE MONTEVIDEO

Un joven periodista cree reconocer a Borges
Perdone señor ¿es usted Borges?
Y el venerable anciano respondió
A veces...

Otra vez alguien tocó el timbre de su departamento
Se trata de un señor de unos 30 años
Le informa Norman Thomas di Giovanni
Que en esos días era su secretario

¿Cómo? replica Borges
¿Que todavía queda gente de 30 años?

Así era Borges

Alguien una vez se le acercó
Mientras se paseaba por Florida

Perdone señor Borges
¿Yo le podría hacer una pregunta?

¡Ya la hizo!
Respondió el venerable anciano
Y apuró el paso

LXVII

ONCE ON MONTEVIDEO AVENUE

A young journalist believes he recognizes Borges
Pardon me sir, Are you Borges?
And the venerable old man replied
Some of the time...

On another occasion someone rang his apartment bell
It's a man of about 30 years of age
He's told by Norman Thomas di Giovanni
Who in those days was his secretary

How so? replies Borges
Are there still people 30 years old?

That was Borges

One time someone approached him
While he was strolling through the Florida quarter

Excuse me Mr. Borges
Could I ask you a question?

You already have!
Responded the venerable old man
And hurried away

LXVIII

HIJO MÍO

                         defraudas a tu madre
Fue para Rey que te engendró tu padre
No para presidente
                         déjate de pamplinas

Si no fueras tan loco te aseguro
Que ya serías el Monarca Absoluto

Emperador o nada por favor!

LXVIII

MY DEAR SON

               you've disappointed your mother
Your father begot you to be a King
Not a President
             stop fooling around

If you weren't so crazy I assure you
By now you'd be an Absolute Monarch

An emperor please or nothing else!

LXIX

CONSEJOS A S.E.

Ninguno
Quién soy yo para andar en esos trotes

Sólo recordaré que la Moneda
Se hizo para perder el tiempo
Claro que de la manera + provechosa posible

El Monarca Absoluto
Tiene la obligación de tratar a sus súbditos
Como si fueran miembros de la Familia Real
Más aún:
Como si fueran miembros de su propio cuerpo

Petrarca dixit

& last but not least
Nadie debe ganar + que Su Excelencia
       el Presidente de la República

Ni—dijolotro

LXIX

ADVICE FOR H.E.

None
Who am I to be giving any

I'll only recall that the Presidential Palace
Was made for wasting time
For certain in the most profitable way possible

The Absolute Monarch
Has an obligation to treat his subjects
As if they were members of the Royal Family
Even more:
As if they were members of his own body

Petrarch said

& last but not least
Nobody should earn more than His Excellency
                              the President of the Republic

Not even—as so-and-so said

LXX

QUERIDA MAMACITA

No importa que te hayas muerto
Estoy seguro que volveremos a vernos
Y que volveré a mamar de tu leche

Soy tu hijo verdad?
                    y seguiré siéndolo
Mientras no se demuestre lo contrario

LXX

MOTHER DEAR

It doesn't matter that you have died
I'm certain that we shall see one another again
And that once more I will suckle your milk

I am your son am I not?
                              and will go on being so
Till it's proved otherwise

LXXI

CÁCERES* LO TENÍA POR AVARO

No nos dejaba tocar la vitrola
So pretexto de que los discos se rayan

Y Lafourcade sostiene que el infarto
Se produjo x no pagar un taxi
De la estación de Cartagena a su casa
Que está en la punta del cerro

*Jorge

LXXI

CÁCERES* TOOK HIM FOR A MISER

He wouldn't let us play the victrola
Under the pretext the records would get scratched

And Lafourcade contends that his heart attack
Was brought on by not paying for a taxi
From the station at Cartagena to his house
That sits at the top of the hill

*Jorge

LXXII

ME IDENTIFICO PLENAMENTE CON ÉL

Hay que cuidar los discos
Y la salud

Imprescindible
Caminar un poco todos los días

A medianoche tanto mejor

En lo posible con la ✝ a cuestas

LXXII

I IDENTIFY WITH HIM COMPLETELY

One has to take care of one's recordings
And one's health

It's essential
To walk a little every day

Even better in the middle of the night

And if at all possible carrying a ✝

LXXIII

NO ERA NINGÚN ATLETA

Hay que imaginárselo físicamente débil
Y de no muy elevada estatura
Cargando como burro con sus maletas
A mediodía bajo un sol infernal
Enero 1948
Pero lo que es más grave
        De cuello y corbata
De terno gris y de sombrero negro

LXXIII

HE WASN'T ATHLETIC AT ALL

One has to imagine him as physically frail
And in stature not very tall
Lugging his suitcases like a pack animal
At midday under an infernal sun
January 1948
But what is even more deadly
                    with collar and necktie
In dark suit and black hat

LXXIV

ÚLTIMA HORA-URGENTE

Las golondrinas de Altazor
Andan revoloteando x aquí

Ven? Ahí pasa una a ras de suelo!

LXXIV

FLASH—BREAKING NEWS

Here the swallows of Altazor
Go flitting about

See? There's one grazing the ground!

LXXV

TUVO RAZÓN EL BÚHO CUANDO DIJO

Que no deberíamos seguir bostezando
Como si Huidobro no hubiera existido
Basta mirar los títulos
De sus escritos múltiples en francés
Para ver los puntos que calza:
Tour Eiffel
                    Horizon Carré
                                        Tout à Coup
Etc. etc.

Claro
Se le moteja de extranjerizante
Por el delito de haber sido bilingüe

¡Como todo burgués que se respete no +!

Lo terrible del caso
Es que resultó ser el + chileno de todos
Algo
Que no debiera sorprender a nadie
Por la sencilla razón
De que escribe prácticamente como se habla
A pesar de su propia teoría
Que no podía ser más vanguardista
En el peor sentido de la palabra:

Piedras preciosas ni regaladas

LXXV

THE OWL WAS RIGHT WHEN HE SAID

We shouldn't go on yawning
As if Huidobro had never existed
Quit looking at the titles
Of his multiple writings in French
To tell how intelligent he was:
Tour Eiffel
            Horizon Carré
                        Tout à Coup
Etc. etc.

Sure
He's nicknamed a lover of foreign ways
For the crime of having been bilingual

Like any bourgeois with self-respect!

The worst thing is
That he turned out to be the most Chilean of all
Something
That shouldn't come as a surprise to any
For the simple reason
That he practically writes the way he speaks
In spite of his own theory
Which couldn't be more vanguardist
In the worst sense of the word:

Precious stones not even as a gift

Estoy pensando en sus mejores poemas
En sus famosos Últimos Poemas
Y también en su texto autobiográfico
Que sólo puede compararse me parece a mí
Con la segunda Carta del Vidente
Léase Vicente

I have in mind his better poems
His famous Last Poems
And also his autobiographical text
That can only be compared it seems to me
With the Second Letter of the Seer
Of Vicente I mean

LXXVI

ME QUEDO CON HUIDOBRO

Declara la Contraloría General de la República:

Los demás me parecen excelentes
Pero no me enloquecen en absoluto

Comienza mal
                    pero termina bien

Ningún niño prodigio

Otros hacen el recorrido al vésre:

Puede que empiecen bien
pero terminan como las berenjenas

LXXVI

I'LL STICK WITH HUIDOBRO

The Republic's Chief Accountant declares:

The others seem excellent to me
But I'm not crazy at all about any of them

He begins badly
                              but ends well

No child prodigy

The others do it the other way around:

They may start off fine
But they finish in a mess

LXXVII

ANALFABESTIAS

                      bárbaros
Extraterrestres!:

Demolieron la casa de Huidobro...

LXXVII

ILLITERATE BEASTS

                    barbarians

Extraterrestrials!:

They tore down Huidobro's house…

LXXVIII

SOY

Y estoy con todo los candidatos
Y con c/1 de ellos en particular

Ánimo
          que triunfen todos!
Ésa es mi filosofía política!

No me pidan que firme x uno solo
Salvo que se llame Carlos Ibáñez del Campo

LXXVIII

I AM

And remain on the side of all the candidates in general
And with each 1 of them in particular

Cheer up!
                    may you all win!
That is my political philosophy

Don't ask me to sign up for only one
Unless his name is Carlos Ibáñez del Campo*

*Translator's note: Chilean military dictator during part of 1931, referred to
 again on page 431.

LXXIX

OPINIÓN PERSONAL:

Uno de los pocos poetas chilenos
Que se deja leer de corrido

Lo que no sucede
Con la gran mayoría de los plumíferos
Es una bieja bieja historia
Según la fonética del Maestro Isaías Cabezón:

Hay que leer de atrás para adelante
De lo contrario no sucede mucho

LXXIX

PERSONAL OPINION:

One of the few Chilean poets
Who can easily be read straight through

What happens
With the vast majority of scribblers
Is an auld auld story
According to the phonetics of Master Isaías Cabezón:

One has to read from back to front
Any other way won't come to much

LXXX

NO SOY TAN PARRANOICO

Como para pensar
Que Huidobro es el hoyo del queque
Perro me consta que es autor imprescindible
En la bibliografía de todo poeta joven
Y de todo lector que se respete
Para decirlo todo de una vez

LXXX

I'M NOT SO PARRANOID

As to think
That Huidobro's the cat's pajamas
But I'll be dogged if he's not a required author
In the bibliography of every young poet
And of every reader who's worth his salt
To say it once and for all

LXXXI

SU MONUMENTO AL MARX HA ENVEJECIDO

Lo sé
Gracias
A los buenos oficios del Consumismo
No tanto como las Églogas de Garcilaso x suerte
(Puras corrientes aguas cristalinas)
El marx de Cartagena aún se sigue estrellando
Contra los arrecifes de la costa
Contaminado
                    pero mar al fin

LXXXI

HIS MONUMENT TO MARX HAS DATED

I know
Thanks
To the good offices of Consumerism
Luckily not so much as the Eclogues of Garcilaso
(Pure currents crystalline waters)
The marx of Cartagena keeps crashing
Into the coastal reefs
Contaminated
            but still the sea

LXXXII

EN FIN

Él fue quien puso la primera piedra
Como también la antepenúltima
De ese edificio llamado Poesía Chilena Nueva
Cuando Neftalí Reyes
Aún no se había cambiado de nombre

Eran los días de la Primera Guerra Mundial
Eran las noches de la Segunda Guerra Mundial

Él bajó de su torre de marfil
Él dijo nones
A toda forma de tontalitarismo

Que lo diga el teléfono de Hitler

LXXXII

FINALLY

It was he who lay the first stone
As well as the next to last
Of that edifice designated New Chilean Poetry
When Neftalí Reyes
Had not yet changed his name

Those were the days of the First World War
Those were the nights of the Second World War

He came down from his ivory tower
Said nay
To every form of totalitaridiocy

The proof is in Hitler's telephone*

---

*Translator's note: Parra is referring to Huidobro's claim that he owned Hitler's telephone. In his *Obras públicas*, Parra reproduces a type of field telephone that soldiers cranked for making a call. The image bears a caption that reads: "El teléfono de Hitler. Colección Vicente Huidobro" ("Hitler's telephone. Collection of Vicente Huidobro"). The earlier reference to Neftalí Reyes is to the real name of Pablo Neruda.

LXXXIII

PASARON ESOS TIEMPOS

Vinieron otros peores
Hoy estamos de vuelta de todos los archipiélagos
O de casi todos
El respetable público dirá
Aprendida la lección de Huidobro
Los Centenarios cuando no dan vida matan
Fin al enfrentamiento
Quiero creer que ése es su mensaje
Mensaje de mensajes
Enfrentamiento
                  sinónimo de extinción

LXXXIII

THOSE TIMES ARE GONE

Worse came along
Today we're back from all the archipelagos
Or almost all
The respectable public will decide
Huidobro's lesson learned
When Centennials don't bring life they kill*
End of confrontation
I wish to believe that's his message
Message of messages
Confrontation
                    synonymous with extinction

*Translator's note: Parra is alluding to a line in Huidobro's poem, "Ars poética": "El adjetivo, cuando no da vida, mata" ("The adjective, when it does not give life, kills").

LXXXIV

Paz sobre la constelación cantante de las aguas
Entrechocadas como los hombros de la multitud
Paz en el mar a las olas de buena voluntad
Paz sobre la lápida de los naufragios
Paz sobre los tambores del orgullo y las pupilas tenebrosas
Y si yo soy el traiductor de las olas
Paz también sobre mí

Las Cruces, 3 de septiembre de 1993

LXXXIV

Peace over the singing constellation of waters
Colliding as shoulders of the multitude
Peace in the sea to the waves of good will
Peace upon the shipwrecks' memorial stones
Peace be to the drums of pride and the darksome pupils
And if I am the transla(trai)tor of the waves
Peace also to me

Las Cruces, 3 September 1993

DISCURSO DEL BÍO BÍO

BÍO BÍO SPEECH

I

HASTA AQUÍ LOS DISCURSOS HAN SIDO BUENOS

Pero largos
El mío será malo qué duda cabe
Pero corto

Me propongo pasar a la reserva
Como el orador + lacónico de la tribu

Para decirlo todo de una vez
Advertiré que mi discurso consta de una sola palabra:
Gracias señor Rector
Es un honor muy grande para mí
Inmerecido por donde se mire:
En esto sí que soy intransigente
He dicho

BÍO BÍO SPEECH

I

UP TO NOW THE SPEECHES HAVE BEEN GOOD

But long
My own will no doubt be bad
But brief

I intend to end up second string
As the most short-winded speaker on the team

Once and for all
I will inform you that my talk consists of just one word:
Thanks, Mr. President
It's a very great honor for me
Undeserved any way you look at it:
On this point yes I am unyielding
I have had my say

II

LA PRIMERA VEZ QUE PASÉ POR AQUÍ

De ésto hace una porrada de años
Fue en condición de lazarillo de un vendedor ambulante
Frutas
      verduras
            útiles de escritorio
Perlina y radiolina

No olvidaré jamás ese canasto de mimbre

Tendría unos 12 ó 13 años
Estaba en el 2º o 3º Año de Humanidades
En el Liceo de Chillán...

Ahora soy Doctor Honoris Causa caramba
Good bye to all that
Gozo de la confianza de algunos filósofos
El Oráculo tenía razón
Cambia todo cambia
Sólo la Dictablanda permanece

II

THE FIRST TIME THAT I CAME THROUGH HERE

It's been a bunch of years since then
I was working as a guide for a blind traveling salesman
Fruits
            vegetables
                        writing supplies
Pearl detergent and Radio brand

I will never forget that wicker basket

I would have been 12 or 13
In the 2nd or 3rd year
Of Chillán middle school…

Now I'm an Honorary Doctor gracious me
Good bye to all that
I have the support of certain philosophers
The Oracle was right
All things change
Only the Milddictatorship remains the same

III

LOS HINDÚES SON GENTE DE CUIDADO

(Déjenme comenzar con esta frase)
La Madre Tierra nó
Qué estupidez eso de las raíces
Oxford & Cambridge!
¡Londres! es lo que cuenta para ellos

England
My Dictionary!
T.S. Eliot el tema x excelencia
Después de esta vi(ud)a no hay otra

III

THE HINDUS ARE A DANGEROUS PEOPLE

(Let me start with this phrase)
Mother Earth no
What stupid business all that about roots
Oxford & Cambridge!
London! is what counts for them

England
My Dictionary!
T.S. Eliot's preeminent theme
After this widowlife there is no other

IV

NO PODEMOS QUEJARNOS DE ESCASEZ DE DOCTORES

Que lo digan los Padres de la Inglesia
Santo Tomás Doctor Angélico
San Agustín Doctor de la Gracia
San Buenaventura Doctor Seráfico
San Bernardo Doctor Melifluo
Raimundo Lulio Doctor Iluminado
Guillermo de Occam Doctor Invencible
Gregorio de Rimini Doctor Auténtico
Juan Gerson Doctor Cristianísimo

Para no mencionar al Doctor Faustus
Que le entregó su alma a Satanás
A cambio de un puñado de conocimientos

IV

WE CAN'T COMPLAIN ABOUT A SCARCITY OF DOCTORS

Just to name the Churchgroin Fathers
Saint Thomas Angelic Doctor
Saint Augustine Doctor of Grace
Saint Buenaventura Celestial Doctor
Saint Bernard Sweet-Tongued Doctor
Raimundo Lulio Enlightened Doctor
William of Occam Invincible Doctor
Gregory of Rimini a Real Doctor
Juan Gerson a Very Christian Doctor

Not to mention Doctor Faustus
Who sold his soul to the Devil
In exchange for a handful of facts

V

EXPLOSIÓN DEMOGRÁFICA DE DOCTORES

El Dr. Lenz
Iniciador de los estudios antropológicos en este país
El Dr. Oroz
El Dr. Salas
Candidato a la Presidencia de la República
Salas Sale Solo
El Dr. Nicolai & el Dr. Lipschutz
Enemigos políticos irreconciliables
Se garabateaban en latín
En el Salón de Honor de la U
Década del 40
Parecían 2 energúmenos del siglo XIV
Tiempos aquellos
& el Dr. Salvador Allende Gossens
El + caro de todos los Doctores

V

POPULATION EXPLOSION OF DOCTORS

Dr. Lenz
Originator in this country of anthropological studies
Dr. Oroz
Dr. Salas
Candidate for President of the Republic
Salas sails solo
Dr. Nicolai & Dr. Lipschutz
Irreconcilable political enemies
They cursed one another in Latin
In the University's Hall of Honor
During the '40s
They seemed like 2 14th-century wild men
Those olden times
& Dr. Salvador Allende Gossens
The dearest most costly Doctor of all

VI

A LA PALABRA DOCTOR

Se le adjudican al menos los siguientes significados
1. Alguien que conoce bien su materia
2. Alguien que tiene algo que decir
3. Una voz que viene de lejos
4. Uno que hace hablar a las estatuas
5. Alguien que habla sin mover los labios
6. Un espectro que se ríe de todo
Incluida la demostración ontológica de la ∃ de Marx
7. Sombra que se desplaza x la Biblia
Como don Pedro Aguirre Cerda x su casa de Conchalí

Me quedo con el sentido
Que le asigna la Commedia Dell'Arte
Dos puntos
Personaje grotesco
Caricatura de universitario pedante
Se le reconoce x sus discursos retóricos interminables
Plagados de citas greco-latinas
En Chile quiere decir matasano
Comúnmente se usa como sinónimo de Jefe
En sentido burlesco:
Hola Doctor
Hola Maestro Hola Jefe
Tratar a alguien de Dr. en Chile
Es casi tan grave como sacarle la madre
Que la verdad no quede sin ser dicha

VI

TO THE WORD DOCTOR

Are assigned at least the following meanings
1. Someone who knows his subject well
2. Someone who has something to say
3. A voice that comes from afar
4. One who makes statues speak
5. Someone who talks without moving his lips
6. A phantom who laughs at everything
Including the ontological demonstration of the Existence of
    Marx
7. Shadow that moves through the Bible
Like President Pedro Aguirre Cerda through his house in
                                    Conchalí

I stick to the meaning
Assigned by the Commedia Dell' Arte
Quote
Grotesque character
Caricature of a university pedant
Recognized by his interminable rhetorical orations
Loaded with Greek and Latin citations
In Chile it signifies kill the healthy
Commonly used as a synonym for Boss
In a burlesque sense:
Hello Doc
Hello Honcho Hello Chief
To call one Dr. in Chile
Is almost as serious as insulting his mother
Let the truth be told

VII

PARA SERLES SINCERO

Yo tenía un temor patagüino
A que alguna vez se me declarara doctor
Ahora veo que no es nada del otro mundo
Todo lo contrario
Algo perfectamente natural
Como nacer
Como contraer matrimonio
Como tener hijos
Y por qué no decirlo:
                            como morir

Tengo la sensación
De que en estos precisos momentos
Estoy emergiendo del vientre materno
Música maestro!

No se diga que son mis funerales
Olvídense!
Vivo no me pondrán en el ataúd
Al cementerio x mis propios pies

VII

TO BE STRAIGHT WITH YOU

I was scared to death
That some day I would be made a doctor
Now I see that it's nothing out of the ordinary
On the contrary
Something perfectly natural
Like being born
Like getting married
Like having kids
And why not say it:
                          like dying

I have a sense
That at this very moment
I am emerging from the maternal womb
Music maestro!

Don't think this is my funeral
Forget it
They won't put me in the coffin alive
I'm going to the cemetery on my own two feet

VIII

BROMAS APARTE

Qué se hace en un caso como éste
Yo Doctor Honoris Causa?
Yo profeta en mi tierra?
Permítanme que me sonría…
Tomadura de pelo + grande no hay
Faltan palabras en el diccionario
Los lugares comunes de rigor
Acuden como moscas al antipoema
Lo mejor será quedarse callado
Me consolaré pensando
Que de poeta
     de doctor
       & de loco
Todos tenemos un poco
Según reza la lira popular

VIII

JOKING ASIDE

What does one do in a case like this
I an Honorary Doctor?
I a prophet in my own land?
Let me crack a smile…
This is the biggest leg pull ever
There aren't enough words in the dictionary
The usual commonplace topics
Are drawn like flies to the antipoem
The best thing to do is keep my mouth shut
I'll console myself with thinking
That of poet
                    of doctor
                                    & of madman
We all are a little compacted
As the popular lyric has it

IX

NO COMETERÉ LA TORPEZA

De rechazar elogios inmerecidos
El cuero no me da para tanto

Soy humano lo reconozco
Los acepto de mil amores
Pero los considero exagerados

IX

I WON'T BE SO STUPID

As to reject undeserved eulogies
I'm not about to do that

I'm human I recognize it
I accept them with all my heart
But do consider them exaggerated

X

UNA SOLA PREGUNTA

Cuándo piensan erigirme una estatua
Ya estaría bueno
La paciencia también tiene su límite
Sin estatua me siento miserable
Pero x favor que sea de barro
Para que dure lo menos posible
Yo soy un hombre que ha sufrido mucho
Más de lo que delatan las arrugas
Sólo creando mundos me consuelo

¿Lagunas mentales?
No se preocupe
Péguese un viajecito a la Argentina
Se las quitarán de inmediato

X

JUST ONE QUESTION

When do you plan to erect a statue of me
Right now would be a good time
Patience also has its limits
I would feel miserable without a statue
But please let it be of clay
So it'll last as short a time as possible
I am a man who has suffered much
More than my wrinkles betray
Only creating worlds consoles me

Mental lapses?
Don't worry
Take a little trip to Argentina
They will fix them up right away

XI

ME PREGUNTAN QUE SI DE VOLVER A NACER

Volvería a escribir lo que he escrito
Por supuesto Sras & Sres
Claro que reservándome el derecho
A modificar el fondo & la forma
Lo único que conservaría tal cual
Es el título de las Obras Completas
Opera Omnia
Basura para Todos

& la Dedicatoria:
A Dios
Exista o no exista

XI

THEY ASK ME IF I WERE TO BE BORN AGAIN

Would I write once more what I have written
By all means Ladies & Gentlemen
Of course reserving to myself the right
To modify the form & content
The only thing that I would keep the same
Is the title the Complete Works
Opera Omnia
Garbage For Everyone

& the Dedication:
To God
Whether He exists or not

XII

¿FIN DE LA HISTORIA?

Me desayuno
Cómo va a terminar
Algo que no comienza todavía…

XII

THE END OF HISTORY?

I don't know
How is something going to end
When it hasn't even begun...

XIII

QUÉ PASA!

Veo que están bostezando:
No importa
Bienaventurados los que tienen sueño
Porque no tardarán en quedarse dormidos

XIII

WHAT'S WRONG!

I see that you are yawning:
Doesn't matter
Blessed are the sleepy
For they shall soon be sound asleep

XIV

ÚLTIMA HORA URGENTE

El Sr. Decano me informa
Que mi grado académico me faculta
Para pedir lo que se me antoje
Medallón de perfil en la sala de espera
Busto de mármol en el Correo Central
Estatua ecuestre en el Asilo de Ancianos

Honor & Gloria
A los veteranos del 69!

Me conformaré con una placa recordatoria
Que diga

> En esta casa parduzca
> Vive el traductor de Dante
> Apúrate caminante
> No sea que te traduzca

XIV

FLASH BREAKING NEWS

The Dean informs me
That my academic degree authorizes me
To ask for whatever I wish
A large medallion in profile in the waiting room
A marble bust in the Main Post Office
An equestrian statue in the Old Folks Home

Honor & Glory
To the veterans of 69!

I'll be satisfied with a memorial plaque
Which would state

> In this grayish abode
> Lives Dante's translator
> Hurry on by traveler
> Or he'll break your code

XV

NO SOY TAN PARRANOICO

                        después de todo
Como para creer que gracias a este birrete
Se me abrirán las puertas del celebro:
Ya lo dijo la tía de mi tía:
Lo que natura non da
Salamanca non convida

Pero de algo sí que estoy seguro:
De hoy en adelante
Mis nietos psicodélicos
Van a tener que pensarlo 2 veces
Antes de avergonzarse del abuelo

Conviene recordarlo:
No tengo nada contra las sandías
Son los melones los que yo no soporto

XV

I'M NOT SO PARRANOID

                    after all
As to believe that thanks to this academic cap
The doors of my mind will be opened:
The aunt of my aunt has already said it:
That which nature hasn't given
Salamanca cannot confer

But of one thing I am positively certain:
From now on
My psychedelic grandchildren
Are going to have to think twice
Before feeling ashamed of grandpa

It's fitting to recall:
I have nothing against watermelons
It's just the melons that I cannot stand

XVI

OTRA PREGUNTA DIGNA DE RESPUESTA

Me podrían decir quién inventó
La llamada Dialéctica Socrática?

Alguien anda diciendo x ahí que no fue Sócrates
Sino la Doctora Fantasma:
Aspasia
Su Profesora de Filosofía:
La cortesana + hermosa de todas

Ojo con esa mujer!

Ella sería también la autora
Del famoso Discurso de Pericles

Ojo pestaña & ceja
Con esa vieja

XVI

ANOTHER QUESTION DESERVES AN ANSWER

Can you tell me who invented
The so-called Socratic Dialogue?

Someone around here's been saying it wasn't Socrates
But rather Doctor Phantom:
Aspasia
His Professor of Philosophy:
The most beautiful whore of all

Watch it with that woman!

She would also be the author
Of the famous Speech of Pericles

Keep your eyes peeled
Careful with that crone

XVII

UN HETEROSEXUAL INTRANSIGENTE

No podrá jamás acceder
A los misterios propiamente tales
De la nunca bien ponderada cultura helénica
Según el autor de *Los Alimentos Terrestres*

Sólo para Platón & Cía.
Fueron condimentados esos manjares

Los mortales vulgares & silvestres
Tendremos que conformarnos
Con chuparnos el dedo
Salvo que se nos dé vuelta el paraguas

Que la verdad no quede sin ser dicha

XVII

AN INTRANSIGENT HETEROSEXUAL

Will never be able to consent
To the mysteries properly such
Of the never well-pondered Hellenic culture
According to the author of *The Earthly Nourishment*

Only for Plato & Co.
Were those dishes seasoned to taste

We vulgar & uncultivated mortals
Will have to content ourselves
With what we have
Unless we switch to the other team

Let the truth be told

XVIII

PROYECTOS?

Claro que sí!
Me propongo pasar a la reserva
Como el tra(i)ductor de Hamlet
Al mapudungún

No como poeta ni como antipoeta

Pasaron esos tiempos calamitosos
Uf!
Después del escándalo del Rey Lear
¡114 funciones consecutivas a tablero vuelto!
Me considero con derecho a todo

Lo malo es que los auspiciadores
No se divisan x ninguna parte

That is the question

XVIII

PLANS?

Yes I certainly do have some!
I intend to keep a low profile
As the transla(trai)tor of Hamlet
Into the Mapuche tongue

Not as a poet nor an antipoet

Those calamitous times are over & done
Whew!
After the King Lear scandal
114 straight sold-out performances!
I consider myself entitled to everything

The trouble is that promoters
Can't be spotted in any direction

That is the question

XIX

CONSEJOS TEÓRICOS & PRÁCTICOS

1

Escriban lo menos posible
Preferible sentir a verbalizar
& solamente en el idioma patrio

2

Orinen de pie
De espaldas a la cordillera

3

Vivienda
A una altura mínima de 50 mts
Sobre el nivel del marx

4

Megadosis de ácido ascórbico
Natural
El artificial es cancerígeno

5

Precaución en caso de maremoto
Pedir auxilio al Puesto de Policía más próximo
Salvo indicación en contrario

XIX

THEORETICAL & PRACTICAL ADVICE

1

Write as little as possible
It's better to feel than to verbalize
& only in the native tongue

2

Pee standing up
With your back to the cordillera

3

Housing
at a minimum height of 50 meters
above the level of the marx

4

Megadose of natural
ascorbic acid
the artificial type is carcinogenic

5

Take precautions in case of a tidal wave
Seek aid from the nearest Police Station
Unless otherwise instructed

6

Cristianismo claro que sí
Pero lúdico
En oposición amistosa al cristianismo autoritario de derecha
y al anticristianismo militante de izquierda

Cero Problema:
La Economía para la Derecha
La Política para la D.C.
Léase Divina Comedia
& la Kurtura para la Clase Trabajadora

7

Arte Poética
1% de inspiración
2 de transpiración
& el resto suerte

Yo es Yo
Yo es Otro
Yo es Nadie
Yo es un muñeco
Yo es la Internet Society
Cuya dirección en el cyberespacio es www.isoc.org

6

Christianity of course
but playfully
in friendly opposition to rightwing authoritarian christianity
and to the militant left's antichristianity

No problem:
Economics for the right
Politics for the Christian Democrats
Read The Divine Comedy
& Kurture for the Working Class

7

Art of Poetry
1% inspiration
2 of transpiration
The rest pure luck

I is I
I is Other
I is Nobody
I is a boy doll
I is the Internet Society
Whose address in cyberspace is www.isoc.org

XX

LA PÁGINA DEPORTIVA

Para meter un gol de mediacancha
Hay que ser un filósofo natural
En toda la extensión de la palabra

Preferible que le den las patadas a la pelota
Antes que se las den entre ellos mismos

Hay que ponerse en órbita compadre

Este es un país de pelotaris:
Hágase futbolista
De lo contrario no le dan pelota

XX

THE SPORTS PAGE .

To kick a goal from midfield
One has to be by nature a philosopher
In the full meaning of the word

It's better that they give the ball a kick
Rather than kicking themselves around

Pal you need to put yourself into orbit

This is a country of show-off jocks:
Become a soccer player
Otherwise they won't give you the time of day*

*Translator's note: The antipoet is playing on the word for ball (*pelota*), which both in Spanish and English carries sports and sexual meanings, but in Spanish it also means "to pay attention to someone" when used in the phrase *darse la pelota*.

XXI

QUE DIJERA ALGO SOBRE LA VEJEZ

Le pidieron una vez sus alumnos
Al Dr. Bertrand Russell
& el venerable anciano respondió

La vejez…
Una edad como cualquier otra
Para luchar x una causa justa

XXI

WOULD YOU SAY SOMETHING ABOUT OLD AGE

His students once asked
Of Dr. Bertrand Russell
& the venerable elder replied:

Old age...
A time like any other
For fighting for a cause that's just

XXII

CAPITALISMO & SOCIALISMO

Economicismos decimonónicos
Anteriores al Principio de Finitud

Ni socialista ni capitalista
Sino todo lo contrario Sr. Director:
Ecologista intransigente

Entendemos x ecologismo
Un movimiento socio-económico
Basado en la idea de armonía
De la especie humana con su medio

Que lucha x una vida lúdica
Creativa
      igualitaria
          pluralista
              libre de explotación

Y basada en la comunicación
Y colaboración de grandes & chicos

XXII

CAPITALISM & SOCIALISM

Nineteenth-century mumbo-jumbo
Prior to the Principle of Finitude

Neither capitalist nor socialist
But just the opposite Mr. Director:
Intransigent ecologist

We understand by ecology
A socioeconomic movement
Based on the idea of the harmony
Between the human species & its environment

Which fights for a ludic life
Creative
        egalitarian
                pluralist
                        free of exploitation

And founded on communication
And collaboration between big & little guys

XXIII

CONSEJOS A SU EXCELENCIA

Ninguno
Quién soy yo para andar en esos trotes

Sólo recordaré
Que La Moneda se hizo para perder el tiempo
Claro que de la manera + provechosa posible

El Monarca Absoluto tiene la obligación
De tratar a sus súbditos
Como si fueran miembros de la Familia Real
Más aún
Como si fueran miembros de su propio cuerpo

Petrarca dixit

& last but not least
Nadie debe ganar + que S.E. el Presidente de la República

Ni – dijolotro

XXIII

ADVICE TO HIS EXCELLENCY

None
Who am I to be trotting out my two-cents' worth

I will only recall
That the Presidential Palace was made for wasting time
Of course in the most profitable way

The Absolute Monarch is obligated
To treat his subordinates
As if they were members of the Royal Family
Even more
As if they were parts of his own body

Petrarch declared

& last but not least
No one ought to earn more than H.E. the President
        of the Republic

Not even – said so-and-so

XXIV

A TODO ESTO CÓMO SE ENTIENDE

Que la Universidad de Concepción
Haya tomado la iniciativa de doctorar
A alguien que no suena ni truena
Ni en su propia casa?

Falta de información:
A la distancia me veo mejor que de cerca
Tengo buen lejos

La Universidad de Chile
No pisará jamás ese palito

Quien no te conozca que te compre
Solía decirle
La pragmática Clara Sandoval
(Dios la tenga en su santo reino)
Al ingenioso Nicanor Parra Parra
Que es el Parra propiamente tal
Antipoeta x derecho propio
Dios lo tenga en su santo reino también
Aleluya!
Si todavía sigue siendo Dios

XXIV

HOW IN THE WORLD COMPREHEND

That the University of Concepción
Has taken it upon itself to make a doctor
Out of a person who no one speaks of or remembers
Not even around his own house?

Lack of information:
I appear better at a distance than up close
I look great from faraway

The University of Chile
Will never fall into that trap

You can fool a stranger
The pragmatic Clara Sandoval
Used to say
(May God keep her in his blessed Kingdom)
As to the ingenious Nicanor Parra Parra
Who is the Parra properly such
Antipoet in his own right
May God also keep him in his blessed Kingdom
Hallelujah!
If He still goes on being God

XXV

BUENO...

Ahora que ya soy Doctor
Dejad que los clientes vengan a mí
Perdón
Dejad que los pacientes vengan a mí
Siempre & cuando no sean de FONASA

Me comprometo bajo palabra de honor
A no cortarle a nadie la pierna sana
En vez de la enferma

Juro x la melena del poeta
No olvidar instrumentos quirúrgicos
En las entrañas de mis parroquianos

Juro no volver a burlar el Séptimo Mandamiento
De N.S.M.I.C.
Salvo caso de extrema necesidad

Desnudar a las pacientas claro que sí
Pero sólo con fines humanitarios
Alabado sea el Santísimo

Mi palabra de honor
Que no cobraré nunca x anticipado
Cheques en blanco muy de tarde en tarde
Guerra a muerte al Negocio de la Salud
Amén

XXV

WELL...

Now that I'm a Doctor
Let the customers come to me
Sorry
Let the patients come to me
As long as they're not under Medicaid

I promise on my word of honor
Not to cut off the healthy limb
Instead of the infirm

I swear by the poet's long hair
Not to leave surgical instruments
Inside my clients' intestines

I promise not to mock the Seventh Commandment
Of NSMIC
Except in a case of extreme necessity

Undress the patients for sure
But only for humanitarian purposes
Praised be the Lord

My word of honor
That I will never charge in advance
Now and again will accept signed blank checks
Will fight to the death against the Health Business
Amen

XXVI

ESO SÍ QUE UNA ADVERTENCIA

A sea quien sea

Depredadores
                    ¡manga de langostas!
Un poquitito de sentido común:

Llévense el cobre
                    llévense el cochayuyo
Llévense los mariscos + deliciosos
La albacora
                    los locos
                                        las centollas
Prácticamente ya no queda nada
Pero cuidado con el bosque nativo carajo:
Se tendrán que batir con los mapuches!

Ésta no es una república bananera
Aquí no hay corrupción
Fuera de la que todos conocemos
Este país es la copia feliz del Edén
O x lo menos una fotocopia

XXVI

BUT A WORD OF WARNING

To whomever it may concern

Ravagers
                    cloud of locusts!
Get a little common sense:

Plunder the copper
                            do away with the seaweed
Sack the most delicious seafood
The albacore
                    the abalone
                                    the spider crabs
They are all practically gone
But damn it watch it with the native woods:
You'll have to answer to the Mapuches!

This isn't a banana republic
There isn't any corruption here
Aside from all that we know about
This country is a happy copy of Eden*
Or at least a photocopy

*Translator's note: The antipoet's phrase, "happy copy of Eden" ("copia
feliz del Edén"), comes from the Chilean National Anthem.

XXVII

CANCIÓN PROTESTA

Alguien anda diciendo x ahí
Que las canciones protesta pasaron de moda
Protesto!

Por lo muy menos hay una
Que no pasará nunca de moda
Para vergüenza del género humano
Música maestro!

Los pollitos dicen
Río Bío Bío
Por que tienen hambre
Porque sienten frío

La gallina busca
El maíz y el trigo
Les da la comida
Y les presta abrigo

Todos!

Bajo sus 2 alas
Acurrucaditos
Hasta el otro día
Duermen los pollitos

XXVII

PROTEST SONG

Somebody is going around here saying
That protest songs are out of fashion
I protest!

At the very least there is one
That never will go out of style
To the shame of the human race
Music maestro!

The chickies cheep
Bío Bío River
From feeling hunger
& beginning to shiver

The hen she scratches
For wheat & corn
Gives them to eat
& keeps them warm

Now all together!

Under her wings
& huddled safe
The chickies sleep
Till break of day

XXVIII

ANTES DE DESPEDIRME

Una buena patada en el hocico
Para el Generalísimo de moda
Por las brutalidades que está cometiendo
Contra la diminuta República de Chechenia

Parecía un gordo buena persona
Pero no es + que un cerdo mofletudo

Nos recuerda los días + negros
Del milenio que está x terminar

XXVIII

BEFORE I TAKE MY LEAVE

A good kick in the snout
For the present Commander in Chief
For the brutalities he's committing
Against Chechnya's tiny Republic

He seemed a fat good-natured guy
But he's just a chubby-cheeked swine

He reminds us of the darkest days
Of the millennium about to end

XXIX

A CONTINUACIÓN

Vienen unas consideraciones impajaritables
Sobre el tema de los derechos humanos
El respetable público dirá
¿Las leo o no las leo?

–Que las lea!

–Tal vez no sea prudente
Se nos podrían ofender las FF.AA.
Léase Ferrocarriles del Estado

Mucho se habla de derechos humanos
Poco
Nada casi sobre deberes humanos
Primer deber humano
Respetar los derechos humanos

XXIX

AND NOW

Here come a few unavoidable thoughts
On the subject of human rights
The respected public will ask
Do I read them or do I not?

–Read them of course!

–Perhaps it wouldn't be prudent
They could offend the Armed Forces
That is the State-run Railway

There's much talk of human rights
Little
Nearly nothing of human responsibilities
The first human responsibility is
To respect human rights

XXX

NO SÉ SI ME EXPLICO

Lo que quiero decir es muchas gracias
A la comunidad académica
De la Universidad de Concepción
Ay!
Se pasó la comunidad académica
Como se ve que estamos en familia
¿No don Augusto?*

Gracias Departamento de Español
Amigos míos incondicionales
Ésta no es la primera vez que nos vemos
Nuestro idilio se remonta a la década del 50
Si la memoria no me es infiel

Los recuerdos se anulan unos a otros
Pero el rumor del río permanece

*Augusto Parra

XXX

I DON'T KNOW IF I MAKE MYSELF CLEAR

What I want to say is many thanks
To the academic community
Of the University of Concepción
Ah me!
The academic community outdid itself
As can be seen we're among family members
Isn't it so Don Augusto?*

Thanks Department of Spanish
My unconditional friends
This isn't the first time we've seen each other:
Our relationship goes back to the 50s
If my memory serves me right

The recollections cancel each other out
But the murmuring of the river remains

*Augusto Parra

XXXI

GRACIAS TITO TRIVIÑOS

Alguna vez me vengaré de ti

Creo tener bien en claro
Lo que esta ceremonia significa:

Premio a la longevidad
Dentro de poco cumpliré los 100
Ultima vez que me presento en público

Después de los sin cuenta
Lo mejor es pasar inadvertido

Gracias Ivette
Gracias María Nieves
Hadas madrinas sin cuyos artilugios
El machitún no creo que hubiera sido posible
Tiempo que Uds. vienen estudiando
Los pormenores de esta poesía
Con una paciencia digna de mejor causa

Alguna vez se arrepentirán

XXXI

THANKS TITO TRIVIÑOS

Some day I'll get even with you

I believe that I know for certain
What this ceremony signifies:

A longevity prize
In not too long I'll turn 100
This will be the last time I'll appear in public

After a certain age
It's better to go unnoticed

Thanks Ivette
Thanks María Nieves
Fairy godmothers without whose contriving
I don't think this gathering would have ever come off
For some time now you have assiduously
Studied this poetry
With a patience worthy of a better cause

One day you'll be sorry you did

XXXII

UN MILLÓN DE GRACIAS

A los oradores
Que me han precedido en el uso de la palabra
A todos los presentes
Y con mayor razón a los ausentes
Sus razones tendrán para no estar aquí
Nada en el mundo ocurre porque sí

Claro que me hubiera encantado
Ver en primera fila
A la Santísima Trinidad de la Chilena Poesía
Madre
       Hijo
            & Espíritu Santo:

A la Mistral
En tenida de monje franciscano

A Neruda
De corbata de rosa y de sombrero alón

A Huidobro
Disfrazado de Cid Campeador

A Magallanes a Pezoa Véliz
Al heroico Domingo Gómez Rojas
(1896-1920)
Está de centenario
A Enrique Lihn   a Eduardo Anguita
Doctores todos x derecho propio

Por + que abro los ojos no los veo

XXXII

A MILLION THANKS

To the orators
Who have spoken before me
To all those present
And even more to the absent
Who will have their reasons for not being here
Nothing in the world happens on its own

Certainly I would have been delighted
To have seen seated in the front row
The holy trinity of Chilean poetry
Father
            Son
                    & Holy Ghost:

Mistral
In her outfit of a Franciscan monk

Neruda
With rose necktie and wide-brimmed hat

Huidobro
Disguised as Cid Campeador

And Magallanes and Pezoa Véliz
Heroic Domingo Gómez Rojas
(1896-1920)
It's his centennial year
& Enrique Lihn   & Eduardo Anguita
All doctors in their own right

No matter how wide I open my eyes I cannot see them

Se me dirá que están en sus poemas
A otro Parra con ese hueso
Lo + probable es que no estén en ninguna parte

Estos
& otros misterios insondables

You'll say they're in their poems
Tell that to another Parra
The most likely thing is they're nowhere

These
& other inscrutable mysteries

XXXIII

EN RESUMEN

en síntesis
en buen romance:

Muchos los problemas
Una la solución:

Economía Mapuche de Subsistencia

XXXIII

IN SUMMARY

    to wrap it up
                to put it plainly:

The problems are many
The solution one:

Mapuche Subsistence Economy

XXXIV

Y PARA TERMINAR...

                por donde debí comenzar
Gracias al Profesor Mario Rodríguez
Al amigo + generoso de todos
Al exégeta
Al Huaso Mario Rodríguez
Motor inmóvil de esta lluvia de flores

Estoy x creer que valió la pena
Apostar a la antipoesía
& perdonen que se me quiebre la voz
Ya les dije que estoy emocionado

XXXIV

AND TO CONCLUDE...

                        where I should have begun
Thanks to Professor Mario Rodríguez
The most generous friend of all
The exegete
The cowhand Mario Rodríguez
Immovable engine of this flower shower

I'm about to believe it was worth the trouble
To place a bet on this antipoetry
& forgive me if my voice begins to shake
I've already said that I'm all choked up

AUNQUE NO VENGO PREPARRADO

THOUGH I HAVEN'T COME PREPARRAED

I

PASÓ LO QUE ME TEMÍA

Los oradores que me han precedido en el uso de la palabra
Han dicho todo
Prácticamente todo lo que se puede decir al respecto
Qué se hace en un caso como éste

No sé

I

WHAT I FEARED WOULD HAPPEN HAS

The speakers who have gone before me
Have said it all
Practically everything that can be said on the subject
What's to be done in such a case

Dunno

II

LO ÚNICO QUE SÉ

Es que estoy en deuda con Luis Oyarzún
Y ni siquiera ésto lo sé muy bien
<u>Estamos</u> en deuda con Luis Oyarzún

El ensayista fuera de serie
El Decano Perpetuo de Bellas Artes
El Director Vitalicio
De la Sociedad de Escritores de Chile
El Viajero Total
El Ministro de Fé de su generación
El Orador Académico por excelencia

II

THE ONLY THING I DO KNOW

Is that I'm indebted to Luis Oyarzún
And not even this do I know very well
<u>We</u> <u>are</u> in debt to Luis Oyarzún

The one in a million essayist
Perpetual Fine Arts Dean
Director for Life
Of the Society of Chilean Writers
The Compleat Traveler
His generation's Minister of Faith
The Academic Orator par excellence

III

LA PRIMERA IMAGEN QUE SE NOS VIENE A LA MENTE

Cuando decimos Luis Oyarzún
Es la del Pensador de Rodin

III

THE FIRST IMAGE THAT COMES TO OUR MIND

When we say Luis Oyarzún
Is The Thinker by Rodin

IV

ERA CAPAZ DE HABLAR DE CUALQUIER COSA

Hasta de fútbol
Si el momento histórico lo requería
Con pleno conocimiento de causa
Hasta con elocuencia parlamentaria
Con un sentido del humor filosófico
Que desarmaba al interlocutor:
Hamlet
        Príncipe de Dinamarca en persona
Claro que con algunos kilos de sobrepeso

IV

HE WASN'T AFRAID TO TALK ABOUT ANYTHING

Even soccer
If the historic moment required it
With complete understanding of the subject
Uttered with parliamentary eloquence
With a philosophic sense of humor
That disarmed the disputant:
Hamlet
      Prince of Denmark in person
Though of course a few pounds overweight

V

EL PEQUEÑO LAROUSSE ILUSTRADO

Le decíamos con mucho cariño
Pues no era muy alto de estatura

La verdad es que sabía + que todos nosotros juntos
Incluído el mismísimo Jorge Millas
A pesar de ser el + joven del grupo
Que contaba además
Con el pintor impresionista Carlos Pedraza
Con el Dr. Hermann Niemeyer
El ingeniero Raúl Montecinos
Especialista en Aguas Subterráneas
Héctor Casanova
Que llegó a Secretario General
De esta Universidad si no me equivoco
& uno que otro + electrón periférico

Para no mencionar a Jorge Cáceres
Que se cortó las venas en el baño

V

LITTLE FRENCH ILLUSTRATED DICTIONARY

We called him with great affection
After all he wasn't very tall

The truth is that he knew more than all of us put together
Including even Jorge Millas himself
In spite of being the youngest of the group
Which included as well
Carlos Pedraza the impressionist painter
Dr. Hermann Niemeyer
Engineer Raúl Montecinos
Specialist in Subterreanean Waters
Héctor Casanova
Later Secretary General
Of this University if I'm not mistaken
& one or two other peripheral electrons

Not to mention Jorge Cáceres
Who slit his wrists in the tub

VI

INBA

Sto. Domingo 3535

Década del 30
Costado norte de la Quinta Normal
Edificio grandote de 2 y 3 pisos
Matucana
Mapocho
todo eso…

Será posible hoy tanta belleza?

Para empezar no teníamos adónde caernos muertos

Por algo nos llamaban los Inmortales

VI

BARROS ARANA NATIONAL INSTITUTE

3535 St. Domingo

Decade of the 30s
North side of Quinta Normal
A huge building of 2 and 3 floors
Matucana
Mapocho
all that...

Would so much beauty be possible today?

To begin with we couldn't even afford to drop dead

No wonder they called us the Immortals

VII

Y COMENZARON A PASAR LAS COSAS

Dictadura de Ibánez
República Socialista de los 100 días
Frente Popular

Era frecuente verlo
Rodeado de jóvenes iconoclastas
En los jardines del Piedragógico
O en la Oficina del Quebrantahuesos:

Tengo orden de liquidar la poesía
Vaca perdida aclara su actitud frente a vaca encontrada
Alza del pan provoca otra alza del pan

VII

AND THINGS STARTED TO HAPPEN

The dictatorship of Ibáñez
The Socialist Republic of 100 days
The Popular Front

He was often seen
Surrounded by the iconoclastic young
In the gardens of the Pebblegogy*
Or in the Office of the Bonesbreaker:

I have been ordered to liquidate poetry
A lost cow clarifies its attitude in facing a found cow
A rise in bread prices provokes another increase

*Translator's note: "Pebblegogy" is an attempt to render the antipoet's play
on the word *pedagógico* (from the phrase *Instituto pedagógico*, the
University of Chile's pedagogical branch), wherein the Greek *peda* or
paeda (a slave who led children to school) has been changed in the
Spanish to *piedra* (meaning rock, stone or pebble). Although the poem's
specific reference would seem to be to 1931 and the dictatorship of Carlos
Ibáñez del Campo, the word *piedragógico* still applies to student activists
(or iconoclasts) who pile up rocks on campus and throw them at the police
and their *guanacos* (water cannons named for the Chilean camel-like
creature who spits as a form of defense).

VIII

SUS AMIGOS DEL ALMA

Lafourcade
                    Jodorowsky
                                        Lihn

Uno se prendaba de él a primera vista
Pero su sombra fue Roberto Humeres
El pintor
                    el flanneur
                                        el dandy
Que acababa de volver de París:
Roberto Humeres Solar
El Fantasma del Buque de Carga
Corruptor de menores & Mayores

VIII

HIS SOUL MATES

Lafourcade
        Jodorowsky
                Lihn

One took to him right away
But his shadow was Roberto Humeres
The painter
        the flanneur
                the dandy
Just returned from Paris:
Roberto Humeres Solar
Ghost of the Freighter
Corrupter of young & Old

IX

EN MATERIA POLÍTICA

Se le recuerda x sus ideas eclécticas

Era un hombre común & corriente
En el buen sentido de la palabra
Lo tiene:
Sin ilusiones de grueso calibre
Fifty fifty según sus amigos chinos
¿Independiente?

Sería injusto decir que cayó
En el escepticismo acomodático
De los intelectuales
Autodenominados liberales

¿Habrá alguien en Chile me pregunto
Más sexualdemocracia que él?
ATENCIÓN   ¡IMPORTANTE!

IX

IN POLITICAL MATTERS

He is remembered for his eclectic thinking

He was an average Joe
In the best sense of the word
That is:
Without heavy-duty aspirations
Fifty-fifty according to his Chinese friends
Independent?

It would be unfair to say that he fell
Into the accommodating skepticism
Of the self-proclaimed
Liberal intellectuals

Is there anyone in Chile I ask myself
More sexually democratic than he?
ATTENTION   IMPORTANT!

X

NO QUISIERA DEJAR PASAR EL TREN

Sin recordar un artefacto
Que sigue siendo muy ilustrativo
Por obsoleto que pueda parecer a primera vista:

Todas son dictaduras amigo lindo:
Sólo nos está permitido elegir
Entre la de ellos & la de nosotros

X

I WOULDN'T WANT TO LET THE TRAIN PASS BY

Without recalling an artifact
That continues to be quite illustrative
No matter how obsolete it may at first sight seem:

They're all dictatorships my lovely friend:
We are only permitted to choose
Between theirs & ours

XI

ALGUIEN ANDA DICIENDO POR AHÍ

Que en la biblioteca de Luis Oyarzún
Hay un hoyo negro:
Falta Zaratustra
Ein Buch für Alles und Keinen
Un libro para todos & para nadie

Tal vez esa sea la causa
De la penumbra que lo desperfila

Pero díganme Uds. con toda franqueza
Qué escritor chileno de aquella época
Se hizo presente en los funerales de Dios
En serio:
Todos estábamos en la cárcel
Escribiendo poemas incendiarios
Contra la sanguijuela capitalista
Algo que hacía sonreír a Nietzsche
Cuya filosofía social
Parece resumirse en ese viejo proverbio
Que no pasa de moda
Der Wille zur Macht
La Voluntad de Poder:

Independientemente del sistema
Los de arriba se sientan en los de abajo

XI

SOMEBODY IS SPREADING THE RUMOR

That in the library of Luis Oyarzún
There is a black hole:
It lacks Zarathustra
Ein Buch für Alles und Keinen
A book for all & for none

Maybe that's the reason
For the shadows surrounding him

But you tell me in all honesty
Which Chilean writer of that time
Showed up at the funeral of God
Seriously
We were all in jail
Writing incendiary poems
Against the capitalist leech
Something that made Nietzsche smile
Whose social philosophy
Seems summed up in that ancient proverb
Never out of fashion
Der Wille zur Macht
The Will to Power

Regardless of the system
Those above sit on those below

XII

ADMIRADOR INNATO DEL CERRO SAN CRISTÓBAL

Lo remontaba y lo bajaba a pie
En un abatir & cerrar de ojos
Le gustaban los muebles antiguos
Las librerías de segunda mano
Las excursiones a Puchuncaví

Solía detenerse de pronto
A examinar con lupa
Algo que le llamaba la atención
Una flor
        un insecto
                cualquier cosa
Sí señor:
Era un amante de la naturaleza
Algo más:
Un defensor de la naturaleza
Apasionado & lúcido a la vez
En una época de analfabetismo ecológico casi total

¿Esteticista?
            Pero moderado…
¿Modernista?
Como toda la gente de su tiempo
¿Yanacona?
Díganme Uds quién diablo no es un yanacona
Y yo le regalaré una barra de chocolate

Que levanten la mano
Los pobladores propiamente tales
Escepciones las hay pero no muchas

XII

BORN ADMIRER OF SAN CRISTÓBAL HILL

He would climb up & down it
In the twinkling of an eye
He liked antique furniture
Secondhand bookstores
Excursions to Puchuncaví

Often he would suddenly stop
To examine with a magnifying glass
Something that attracted his attention
A flower
    an insect
        whatever

Yes sir:
He was a lover of nature
Even more:
A defender of nature
Passionate & lucid at the same time
In an era of almost total ecological illiteracy

Aesthetician?
    But in moderation...
Modernist?
Like all the people of his day
An outsider?
If you tell me who the devil isn't an outsider
I'll give you a chocolate bar

Raise your hands
Those who are rightfully here
Exceptions there are but very few

XIII

SE MOLESTABA

Se ponía rojo como tomate
Cuando sus desalmados condiscípulos
Le canturreaban en sus propias barbas

[:Todo chico crece:]
Pero el Chico Oyarzún nó

[:Todo chico crece:]
Pero el Chico Oyarzún nó

[:Oh Susana
Que bella es la vida nó:]

Qué compañeros + despistados
Hasta el Teniente Bello queda pálido

XIII

IT BOTHERED HIM

He turned red as a beet
When his cruel fellow students
Hummed in his face

[:Everything little grows:]
But Little Oyarzún no

[:Everything little grows:]
But Little Oyarzún no

[:Oh Susanna
How beautiful is life no:]

What a clueless lot
They are even more lost than Lieutenant Bello

XIV

TIEMPOS AQUELLOS

Todos andábamos como locos
Buscándole la quinta pata
Al gato encerrado:

Lucho fué el único que se la encontró
Palabras textuales
Que lo diga su Diario Íntimo
Calificado por Leónidas Morales
Como una de las grandes configuraciones
De la literatura chilena moderna

Fuera de Enrique Lihn naturalmente

XIV

IN THOSE DAYS

We all went around like lunatics
Looking for the fifth paw
On that cat in the dark:

Lucho was the only one who found it
His exact words
Look them up in his Intimate Journals
Considered by Leónidas Morales
One of the greatest configurations
Of modern Chilean literature

Aside from Enrique Lihn of course

XV

CUANDO NOS ACERCÁBAMOS A FELICITARLO

Porque sus profecías se cumplían
Él contestaba sin inmutarse
Qué le vamos a hacer
                    Soy infalible:

Eríjanme un monumento
& verán cómo me hago famoso

XV

WHEN WE APPROACHED TO CONGRATULATE HIM

Because his predictions had proven true
He calmly responded
What can I tell you
                    I'm infallible:

Erect me a monument
& see how famous I become

XVI

ASÍ ERA LUIS OYARZÚN

Peña x la madre
El primer metafísico del Mapocho
Que es el verdadero nombre de Santiago de Chile
El nombre que tenía
A la llegada de los invasores

La Mistral lo quería como a un hijo

Nos deslumbraba con sus ocurrencias

XVI

LUIS OYARZÚN WAS LIKE THAT

Peña on his mother's side
The first metaphysician of the Mapocho
Which is the authentic name of Santiago Chile
The name that it had
When the invaders arrived

Mistral loved him like a son

He dazzled us with his wit

XVII

COMO SI TODO ESTO FUERA POCO

Fué también un Bohemio de Jornada Completa

Que lo digan los muchachos del Bosco
Los soñadores del Café Iris
Los insomnes del Parque Forestal
& muy en particul(i)ar
Los incorregibles noctámbulos madrugadores
De la Posada del Corregidor
Entre los cuales nos contamos todos

XVII

AS IF THIS WERE NOT ENOUGH

He was also a full-time Bohemian

Listen to the boys of the Bosco
The dreamers of the Café Iris
The insomniacs of Parque Forestal
& a(s)specially
The incorrigible night-wanderers till dawn
From the Inn of the Chief Magistrate
Among whose number we all belonged

XVIII

SONETOS EN COLABORACIÓN

Uno de sus deportes favoritos

XVIII

COLLABORATIVE SONNETS

One of his favorite sports

XIX

¿REPAROS?

Uno que otro:
No era un esquizofrénico
Mal negocio no ser esquizofrénico
Para alguien que aspira a decir algo

No sé si me explico:
Demasiada facilidad de palabra
Falta sorpresa Falta disparate
Todo está en el lugar que le corresponde
Canta como es debido
Pero desde el interior de una jaula

Tiene + de terrestre que de extraterreste

Su perfección marmórea lo perjudica

XIX

CRITICISMS?

One or two:
He wasn't a schizophrenic
It looks bad not being schizophrenic
For someone who aspires to say something

I don't know if I make myself clear:
Too great a facility with words
Lacks surprise Lacks absurdity
Everything is in its place
Sings just right
But from inside a cage

He has more of the terrestrial than the extraterrestrial

His marmoreal perfection works against him

XX

CLARO QUE

Todo cambiaba como x encanto
Cuando nos poníamos a divagar
Alrededor de una botella de vino
Ni Su Santidad el Obispo de Roma
Escapaba a sus bromas sangrientas

Comillas:
Atrasado de noticias el Sumo Pontífice:
Le falta bibliografía:

Si no redacta de una vez x todas
La Encíclica de la Supervivencia
Voy a tener que redactarla yo

XX

IT'S CLEAR THAT

Everything changed as if by magic
Once we started to ramble on
Around a bottle of wine
Not Even His Holiness the Bishop of Rome
Escaped his brutal jokes

Quotation marks:
The Highest Pontiff's behind the times:
He lacks a bibliography:

If he doesn't draft once and for all
The Encyclical Letter of Survival
I'll have to put it in writing myself

XXI

¿QUE DESTAQUE LO BUENO?

¿Que deje en la penumbra lo problemático?
¿La basura debajo de la alfombra?
¿Realismo socialista otra vez?

Habría que pensarlo 2 veces

XXI

SHOULD I EMPHASIZE WHAT'S GOOD?

Leave what's problematic in the shade?
Sweep the dirt underneath the rug?
Socialist realism all over again?

I'd have to think about it twice

XXII

Y SEGUÍA PASANDO LA PELÍCULA

Radioactividad & Explosión Demográfica
Mariposas en vías de extinción
Narcotráfico
                    Sida
                              Genocidio
Basurales que llegan a la luna

Con excepción de la Torre de Pisa
Todos los monumentos se venían abajo

XXII

AND THE FILM KEPT ROLLING

Radioactivity & Demographic Explosion
Butterflies on the way to extinction
Narcotraffic
                    AIDS
                              Genocide
Garbage dumps reaching to the moon

Except for the Tower of Pisa
All the monuments falling down

XXIII

RUSOS & YANKEES

Economicismos decimonónicos
Anteriores al Principio de Finitud
Depredadores x naturaleza

Poco se gana con el Socialismo
Las fábricas nacionalizadas
Siguen contaminando tanto o + que antes

Aló?
        Con quién hablo…
Tiempo perdido   No contesta nadie

XXIII

RUSSIANS & YANKEES

Nineteenth-century babbling
Prior to the Principle of Finitude
Depredators by nature

Little is gained with Socialism
The industries nationalized
Pollute as much or more than before

Hello?
        With whom am I speaking…
A waste of time   No one answers

XXIV

CATÓLICO PRACTICANTE QUE YO SEPA NO FUÉ

Lo que no debe sorprender a nadie
Nuestros maestros eran
Radicales
       masones
            & bomberos
O socialistas como Eugenio González
Otro Hamlet de luto riguroso
Como Óscar Vera
Traductor impecable del Cementerio Marino:

Zenón
      oh cruel Zenón
            Zenón de Elea
Tú me haz herido con tu flecha alada
Que vuela siempre pero nunca vuela

XXIV

A PRACTICING CATHOLIC SO FAR AS I KNOW HE WAS NOT

Which shouldn't come as a surprise to anyone
Our teachers were
Radicals
  Masons
    & firemen
Or socialists like Eugenio González
Another Hamlet in rigorous mourning
Like Oscar Vera
Impeccable translator of Cemetery by the Sea:

Zeno
  oh cruel Zeno
    Zeno of Elea
You have wounded me with your feathered arrow
Which forever flies yet never flies

XXV

SIN EMBARGO SIGUIÓ EL EJEMPLO DE CRISTO:

No dejó descendencia
Léase no contribuyó a la Explosión Demográfica

No se exilió
Vivió hasta el fin con su sra madre
Como Borges
                como Benjamín Subercaseaux
Haciéndose acreedor
Al epíteto de Hijo Modelo
No completó sus estudios de Leyes
& last but not least
Tuvo la feliz ocurrencia
De morir en Valdivia

Gol de mediacancha!
Ahora le estamos pidiendo que resucite

XXV

STILL HE FOLLOWED CHRIST'S EXAMPLE:

He didn't leave a descendant
That is didn't contribute to the Demographic Explosion

Didn't go into exile
Lived till the end with his lady mother
Like Borges
                like Benjamín Subercaseux
Making himself worthy of
The epithet of Model Son
Didn't complete his studies in Law
& last but not least
Had the bright idea
Of dying in Valdivia

A goal from midfield!
Now we are asking him to come back to life

XXVI

NACIÓ LLAMÁNDOSE LUIS OYARZÚN

Nombre que lo marcó toda la vida
Hasta el momento mismo de su muerte

+ allá de la muerte también

XXVI

HE WAS BORN CALLING HIMSELF LUIS OYARZÚN

The name that marked him for all his days
Right up to the moment of his death

Even beyond it too

XXVII

OTRA HAZAÑA DE LUCHO

Posiblemente la mayor de todas:
Se libró de los cuernos
Gracias
A una genialidad sin precedentes:

Nó a la libreta de matrimonio:
Otra alternativa no hay:

Imposible librarse de los cuernos
Único requisito ser casado
Salvo que uno sea el Rey de Ítaca

Para no ir demasiado lejos
Tomemos el caso de Adán & Eva

XXVII

ANOTHER OF LUCHO'S FEATS

Possibly the greatest of all:
He freed himself from cuckoldry
Thanks
To an unprecedented stroke of genius:

No to the matrimonial record book:
There's no other alternative:

It's impossible to free oneself from the horns
All it takes to have them is getting hitched
Unless one happens to be the King of Ithaca

Not to look any further
Let's take the case of Adam & Eve

XXVIII

PERDONARÁN ESPERO

La pobreza absoluta de metáforas
Es que yo no he venido a Valdivia
A dármelas de poeta
Sino a cumplir con un deber sagrado

No se espere de mí
Literatura a expensas de un amigo

Si esa fuera la idea del jurado
Estoy dispuesto a devolver el Premio

(Aplausos)

XXVIII

YOU WILL FORGIVE I HOPE

My absolute poverty of metaphors
It's because I haven't come to Valdivia
To pose as a poet
But to discharge a sacred duty

Don't expect literature from me
At the expense of a friend

If that was the jury's idea
I'm ready to return the Prize

(Applause)

XXIX

TAREA PARA LA CASA

Árbol genealógico de Luis Oyarzún
Él era bien estricto en esa materia

Muchos de sus parientes
Acostumbraban a veranear en Las Termas
Según expresa & reiterada declaración

Ánimo!

Presidentes no hay en la familia
Pero Primeras Damas claro que sí
Médicos
            Arzobispos
                        Ingenieros

XXIX

HOMEWORK

Luis Oyarzún's genealogical tree
He was very strict in that regard

Many of his relatives
Were used to summering at The Spa
According to express & repeated declaration

Onward & upward!

No Presidents in the family
But First Ladies for sure
Doctors
           Archbishops
                    Engineers

XXX

ÁGAPE EN CASA DE ANTONIO OYARZÚN

Ex profesor de Inglés del Barros Arana
Tío bastante crítico del sobrino
Que x supuesto no figuraba entre los invitados

O nos dejó esperando
                    no recuerdo

Imposible evitar la tentación
Nos dedicamos a descuartizar al ausente:

Poco afectuoso con su señor padre
Demasiado gentil con la mamá
Ha publicado poco últimamente
No se le conoce ninguna polola
No se sabe con mucha exactitud
Dónde pasa los fines de semana
Sospechosamente lampiño
Le convendría dejarse bigote
Debería terminar sus estudios de Leyes

XXX

PARTY IN THE HOME OF ANTONIO OYARZÚN

Former teacher in Barros Arana
An uncle quite critical of his nephew
Who of course was not among the invited

Or he kept us waiting

I don't recall

Impossible to avoid the temptation
We allowed ourselves in cutting down the absentee:

Doesn't show enough affection to his dad
Too gracious with his mom
Lately he has published little
He doesn't have a girl friend
It's not exactly known
Where he spends his weekends
Suspiciously clean-shaven
He would look better letting his moustache grow
He ought to finish his Law degree

XXXI

PARA QUÉ SIRVE LA FILOSOFÍA

Le preguntaron una vez sus alumnos del Piedragógico
& el profeta en su tierra respondió:

Para hacer clases de Filosofía

Se gana poco
                pero se sobrevive

XXXI

WHAT GOOD DOES PHILOSOPHY DO

His students at the Pebblegogy asked him once
& the prophet in his own land replied:

One can give classes in Philosophy

One earns little
              but one survives

XXXII

CHILE ES UN PAÍS DE PELOTARIS

Advierte Luis Oyarzún en su Diario

+ en lo cierto no se puede estar:
Hágase fubolista compadre
De lo contrario no le dan pelota

XXXII

CHILE IS A COUNTRY OF SHOW-OFF JOCKS

Luis Oyarzún declares in his Journal

That couldn't be more true:
Become a soccer player buddy
Otherwise they won't give you the time of day

XXXIII

POLOS OPUESTOS

Yo quería escribir como se habla
En cambio él se sentía muy bien
Hablando
Como quien está leyendo un ensayo de Heidegger

Voz impostada decimos ahora
Pero era el espíritu de la época

50 años de lucha fratricida

XXXIII

EXTREME OPPOSITES

I wanted to write the way one speaks
On the other hand he felt fine
Talking
Like someone reading a Heidegger tract

A trained voice we say today
But it was the spirit of the age

50 years of a fraternal spat

XXXIV

UNA VEZ SE AGARRARON A COSCACHOS

A raíz de la siguiente consideración
Hecha x uno de los contrincantes:

Cristo es un robot
En cambio Lenin es un ser humano

Lucho ganó batalla tras batalla
Pero terminó perdiendo la guerra

Fuimos a dar a la Asistencia Pública
Donde le practicaron respiración boca a boca

Nombre del campeón:
Enrique Lafourcade

XXXIV

ONCE THEY FOUGHT IT OUT BAREKNUCKLED

As a result of the following consideration
Proposed by one of the competitors:

Christ is a robot
Whereas Lenin is a human being

Lucho won battle after battle
But even so he lost the war

We ended up at the Emergency Room
Where they gave him mouth to mouth

The name of the winner:
Enrique Lafourcade

XXXV

TE PARECES A DIOS

Le decía Luis Oyarzún
Al interlocutor indeseable:

Estás en todas partes
& nadie te puede ver

XXXV

YOU SEEM LIKE GOD

Luis Oyarzún told
His unlikable interlocutor:

You are everywhere
& nobody can (stand to) see you

XXXVI

CUANDO MURIÓ JORGE MILLAS

Escribí lo siguiente

Después de una larga y escandalosa persecución
Ha dejado de existir en este país
El profesor Jorge Millas
       El orador
            El poeta
El filósofo Jorge Millas Jiménez
Conceptuado x moros & cristianos
Como el hombre + lúcido de Chile
El + humilde
El + desinteresado
Como también + insobornable
Motivo x el cual
La Dictadura lo privó de su cátedra
Condenándolo a muerte prematura
Por asfixia
       por hambre
           por insomnio
La dignidad en Chile es un delito

Jorge era un búho que no podía vivir
Sino en la caverna de las ideas platónicas

No podemos expresar en palabras
El dolor que nos causa su vía crucis

Hasta cuándo sras y sres!

XXXVI

WHEN JORGE MILLAS DIED

I wrote the following

After a long and scandalous persecution
There has ceased to exist in this country
Professor Jorge Millas
        The orator
             The poet
The philosopher Jorge Millas Jiménez
Deemed by Moors and Christians alike
The most lucid man in Chile
The humblest
The most disinterested
As also the most incorruptible
For which reason
The Dictatorship took away his academic chair
Condemning him to a premature death
By asphyxiation
             by starvation
                    by insomnia
In Chile dignity is a crime

Jorge was an owl who couldn't live
Except in a cave of Platonic ideas

We are unable to express in words
The pain caused in us by his stations of the cross

Ladies and gentlemen how long will this go on!

Y la impotencia para alzar la voz
Y la vergüenza
De no atrevernos a seguir su ejemplo

Sus alumnos de toda la vida
Sus amigos que nunca lo olvidarán

And the impotence for lifting one's voice
And the sense of shame
In not daring to follow his lead

His students of a lifetime
His friends who never will forget him

XXXVII

RIDÍCULO VERDAD?

Todas as cartas de amor são
Ridículas

Não seriam cartas de amor se não fôssem
Ridículas

As cartas de amor, se há amor
Têm de ser
Ridículas

XXXVII

RIDICULOUS ISN'T IT?

All love letters are
Ridiculous

They wouldn't be love letters if they were not
Ridiculous

Love letters, if it is love
Have to be
Ridiculous

XXXVIII

LO QUE OYEN SRAS & SRES

Oyarzún era un ecólogo de infantería
No predicaba
               Sólo practicaba:
Nunca lo ví manejando un vehículo

Se desplazaba a pie x el paisaje
Con su mochila de color temblor

Hasta la bicicleta
Le parecía un crimen contra natura

No sé qué pensarán ustedes
A mí me llama mucho la atención

Nadie menos Padre Gatica que él

XXXVIII

YOU HEARD IT LADIES & GENTLEMEN

Oyarzún was an ecological foot soldier
He didn't preach
          He only practiced:
I never saw him drive a car

He hiked on foot through the countryside
With his earthquake-colored backpack

Even the bicycle
Seemed to him a crime contra naturam

I don't know what you folks think
As for me it really gets my attention

Nobody less like Father Gatica than he*

*Translator's note: Father Gatica appears in a popular refrain as a priest who
  doesn't practice what he preaches: "Padre Gatica que predica pero no
  practica."

XXXIX

EN RESUMEN

En síntesis
En pocas palabras:

Muchos los problemas
Una la solución:

Economía Mapuche de Subsistencia:

Hay que cambiarlo todo de √

O nó dicen Uds...

XXXIX

IN SUMMARY

    In short
In few words:

The problems many
The solution one:

The Mapuche System of Economic Subsistence:
Everything has to be radically changed

Or don't you think...

XL

LA HISTORIA LO ABSOLVERÁ

De acuerdo
Pero la geografía lo dudo

XL

HISTORY WILL ABSOLVE HIM

I agree
But as for geography I doubt it

XLI

¿QUÉ PASARÁ EN EL PRÓXIMO SIGLO?

Vuestro Señor Jesucristo de Elqui no + lo sabe:

La vida humana se duplicará
Cada hombre tendrá 7 mujeres
Se legalizará la pasta base
Pan & cebollas para todo el mundo
Conquistaremos el Santo Sepulcro
Fin a los ataúdes personales
Mínimo 2 cadáveres x tumba
Sursum corda
¡Sauces en el Desierto de Atacama!
¡Cristo de Elqui Presidente de Chile!

XLI

WHAT WILL HAPPEN IN THIS NEXT CENTURY?

The only one who knows is Your Lord Jesus Christ of Elqui:

Human life will be cloned
Each man will have 7 wives
Freebase cocaine will be legalized
Bread & onions for everyone
We will find the Holy Grail
An end to individual coffins
A minimum of two cadavers per tomb
Lift up your hearts
Weeping willows in the Atacama Desert!
Christ of Elqui Chile's President!

XLII

EN QUÉ QUEDAMOS ENTONCES

Esa pregunta ya la contesté:
Escribir como hablan los lectores
& punto

XLII

SO WHAT'S THE DECISION?

I've already answered that question:
To write as readers speak
Period

XLIII

PERO VOLVAMOS A LUIS OYARZÚN

1920-1972

Vivió 52 años
                Igual que Shakespeare
16 años + que la Princesa Diana
40 menos que la Madre Teresa

XLIII

BUT LET US RETURN TO LUIS OYARZÚN

1920-1972

He lived 52 years
 The same as Shakespeare
16 years more than Princess Diana
40 fewer than Mother Teresa

XLIV

UDS SE PREGUNTARÁN

Qué pasó con los otros Inmortales
Prácticamente todos bajo tierra

Si no fuera tan tarde
(Qué hora tienen Uds...)
Pediría un minuto de silencio
Por estos buenos muchachos tan olvidados

Bastante merecido que se lo tienen
Casi todos son Premios Nacionales
Perros Guardianes del Establecimiento
Vergüenza + grande no hay
Nuestro proyecto fué cambiar el mundo
Y el mundo terminó cambiándonos a nosotros

Los que ayer exigían la cabeza del Dictador
Hoy se conforman con verlo mejor peinado

Para llorar a mares

Terminaré pegándome un balazo

XLIV

YOU WILL WONDER

What happened to the other Immortals
Practically all are six-foot under

If it weren't so late
(What time do you have...)
I would ask a minute of silence
For the good old boys so neglected

They deserve it after all
Almost all are National Award winners
Watchdogs of the Establishment
There's no greater embarrassment
Our intention was to change the world
And in the end the world changed us

Those who yesterday called for the Dictator's head
Are content today with seeing it better combed

It makes one weep oceans

I will end up shooting myself

XLV

HAY UN MÉTODO INFALIBLE

Para hacer trabajar gratis a un viejo
Por arruinado o achacoso que esté:

Otorgándole un premio literario
Premio Luis Oyarzún por ejemplo
Que de premio no tiene + que el nombre
Se economiza plata
& se cazan 2 pájaros de un tiro
La vanidad lo devuelve a la vida
Dime que nó Demonio de Alas Negras

XLV

THERE IS A FAIL-PROOF METHOD

For making an old man work for free
No matter how ruined or sickly he be:

Conferring on him a literary prize
For example the Luis Oyarzún Award
It's a prize only in name
It saves money
& kills two birds with one stone
Vanity restores him to life
Isn't that *so* you Black-winged Devil

XLVI

BUENA ONDA LUIS OYARZÚN

Irradiaba una luz ultravioleta

XLVI

RIGHT ON LUIS OYARZÚN

You gave off an ultraviolet light

XLVII

SALUDEMOS EN ÉL AL ARTISTA PRECOZ

Al adolescente de la Plaza Brasil
Al funcionario de cuello & corbata
Al Agregado Cultural de lujo
Pulcro
Conocedor de varios idiomas
Al Eximio Guarén de Biblioteca
Al exégeta de Lastarria
Al fundador de Universidades

& no se diga que es un mal poeta
Luis Oyarzún es un gran escritor
(Un gigante disfrazado de Pulgarcito)
Sin cuyos artilugios
Este machitún no hubiera sido posible

Es un honor muy grande para mí
Gracias x este premio
Tan contundente como inmerecido
Chao   Buenas Noches
Última vez que me presento en público

XLVII

LET US HAIL IN HIM THE PRECOCIOUS ARTIST

The adolescent of Plaza Brazil
The office worker in coat & tie
The deluxe Cultural Attaché
Smartly dressed
Multilinguist
Distinguished Bookworm
The exegete of Lastarria
The founder of Universities

& it can't be said he's a bad poet
Luis Oyarzún's a grand writer
A giant in Tom Thumb disguise
Without whose contrivings
This gathering would not have been

It's a very great honor for me
Thanks for this prize
As meaningful as it's undeserved
So long   Good evening
The last time I'll appear in public

Nicanor Parra was born in 1914 in Chillán, Chile. He studied at Brown University from 1943 to 44 and at Oxford University from 1949 to 1950, before becoming in 1958 Professor of Theoretical Physics at the University of Chile. In 1954 Parra gained international attention as a self-styled antipoet on the publication of his *Poemas y antipoemas*, which in 1966 was issued in the United States by New Directions as *Poems and Antipoems*. During the succeeding decades, Parra published numerous collections of his antipoems, salon verses, *cueca* poems, *artefactos*, sermons, ecological poems, and most recently, in 2006, his *Discursos de sobremesa*, the latter presented here in its first English translation. Winner of two prestigious awards, the Juan Rulfo Prize from Mexico in 1991 and the Reina Sofía Award from Spain in 2001, Parra has long been acknowledged as a major figure in Latin American literature. Critic Harold Bloom has even declared that Parra is undoubtedly one of the best poets of the Western world, as quoted in Parra's *Obras completas & algo +* of 2006. Translators of Parra into English have included a number of outstanding U.S. poets, among them William Carlos Williams, Miller Williams, Thomas Merton, Allen Ginsberg, and W.S. Merwin. Chilean poet-critic Jaime Quezada has commented in his *Nicanor Parra tiene la palabra* (1999) that Parra is "the great Chilean poet, the great national poet. And a [Parra] discourse is profoundly Chilean because it is tied to a form of nationality." Quezada recalls that as early as Parra's *Versos de salón* of 1962 the antipoet had published his "Discurso fúnebre" ("Funeral Address"), and from that same book the critic quotes a five-line stanza in "Lo que el difunto dijo de sí mismo" ("What the Deceased Said of Himself"), by way of indicating that Parra had long been aware of speeches for all kinds of occasions and on all types of subjects, from politics and sports to last words spoken over the deceased or in praise of beneficent persons or institutions. Quezada observes that Parra has especially based his discourses or speeches on those given at gatherings of students or friends after they have had a good deal to drink, suggesting that through these and other forms of often heightened or exaggerated expatiation Parra has turned inside out or reworked a Chilean genre that represents the wit, cynicism, and vehemence of the Chilean people.

Dave Oliphant was born in 1939 in Fort Worth, Texas. He first met Nicanor Parra in 1965, at the antipoet's home in La Reina, on the outskirts of the Chilean capital of Santiago. Oliphant began his career as a translator by rendering into English a few sections of Parra's *La cueca larga* of 1958; later he published translations from Parra's *Otros poemas* (1950-1968), *Palabras obscenas* (1970), and poems printed in the Chilean journal, *Atenea* (1990). In 1999 he translated "Aunque no vengo preparrado," one of Parra's *Discursos de sobremesa*, and in 2007 excerpts from the same collection's "Also Sprach Altazor," with both selections appearing in the literary journal *The Dirty Goat*. Although Oliphant began his translating of poetry in Spanish with the work of Nicanor Parra, he has also translated poems by many other Chilean poets, as well as poetry from other Latin American countries and from the Spanish peninsula. For more than thirty years Oliphant concentrated most of his translating efforts on the poetry of Chilean Enrique Lihn (1929-1988), collecting his Lihn translations in the volume entitled *Figures of Speech* (Host Publications, 1999). Oliphant also translated a 1970 book of poems by Chilean Oliver Welden, entitled in English *Love Hound* (Host Publications, 2006), which won the New York Book Festival's 2007 poetry award. Oliphant's own poetry has been published widely, and two collections of his poems are available from Host Publications: *Memories of Texas Towns & Cities* (2000) and *Backtracking* (2004). Oliphant's most recent book is *Jazz Mavericks of the Lone Star State*, published in 2007 by the University of Texas Press, his third volume on jazz history.